D0142138

Human Resources, Care-giving, Career Progression and Gender

The issue of care-giving is highly pertinent to government thinking and legislation at present in both the UK and the USA, and is of central importance to organisations seeking to adopt family-friendly policies and practices. While much has been written about care-giving, little empirical evidence has been presented in which to ground the debate. This book looks at the relationship between care for dependents and career progression using primary empirical comparative data based on UK and US employee surveys and executive interviews.

The authors show care-giving to be a gender neutral glass ceiling, challenging the traditional perspective of the glass ceiling as the domain of women's careers and working lives. The book demonstrates how the career progress of care-givers depends upon employee time-freedom and how 'family-friendly' policies can and do provoke backlash from unencumbered employees, who may also have high 'outside' priorities in their personal lives.

These findings are located within projections of an ageing population and technological change to argue that individuals, organisations, governments and HR professionals must urgently address the wastage of human potential associated with the role of the care-giver in order to sustain current standards of living. The authors focus upon the role of each stakeholder and outline policy options and strategies for change available to organisations and governments.

This book is essential reading for students and researchers of human resources, those involved in care-giving debates and for human resource professionals and policy makers.

Beulah S. Coyne has more than twenty years of human resources experience in major manufacturing industries. She was the first professional female employed in Labour Relations at Shell Oil's Norco, Louisiana, Refinery Complex. **Edward J. Coyne, Sr.** is a former Fortune's 500 executive and is currently Visiting Professor of Management at Samford University. His experience includes managing major companies in Australia and Jamaica. He is the author of *Targeting the Foreign Direct Investor* (1995). **Monica Lee** is based at Lancaster University, UK. She came to academe from the business world and is now concentrating on mentoring senior managers. She is intrigued by the dynamics around individuals and organisations, and most of her work is about trying to make sense of these.

Routledge Studies in Human Resource Development
Edited by Monica Lee
Lancaster University, UK

HRD theory is changing rapidly. Recent advances in theory and practice, how we conceive of organisations and of the world of knowledge, have led to the need to reinterpret the field. This series aims to reflect and foster the development of HRD as an emergent discipline. Encompassing a range of different international, organisational, methodological and theoretical perspectives, the series promotes theoretical controversy and reflective practice.

Human Resources, Care-giving, Career Progression and Gender

A gender neutral glass ceiling

Beulah S. Coyne, Edward J. Coyne, Sr. and Monica Lee

Routledge
Taylor & Francis Group

LONDON AND NEW YORK

First published 2004
by Routledge
11 New Fetter Lane, London EC4P 4EE

Simultaneously published in the USA and Canada
by Routledge
29 West 35th Street, New York, NY 10001

Routledge is an imprint of the Taylor & Francis Group

© 2004 Beulah S. Coyne, Edward J. Coyne, Sr. and Monica Lee

Typeset in Baskerville by Wearset Ltd, Boldon, Tyne and Wear
Printed and bound in Great Britain by Antony Rowe Ltd,
Chippenham, Wiltshire

All rights reserved. No part of this book may be reprinted or
reproduced or utilised in any form or by any electronic, mechanical,
or other means, now known or hereafter invented, including
photocopying and recording, or in any information storage or
retrieval system, without permission in writing from the publishers.

British Library Cataloguing in Publication Data
A catalogue record for this book is available from the British library

Library of Congress Cataloging in Publication Data
A catalog record for this book has been requested

ISBN 0–415–31856–4

To our families and our friendship

Contents

Figures

Preface

This book represents a journey involving five and a half years of research into the possibilities of reasons for a 'glass ceiling' other than discrimination. The journey began when Professor Monica Lee agreed to accept the challenge of supervising a mature student with a controversial topic. The journey has not been an easy one as both student and supervisor suffered life-threatening illnesses. Both fought back and regained their health, while being cheered on by spouses and family. The Ph.D. was awarded in 2001 and a book suggested. Professor Edward J. Coyne, after living the journey and becoming passionate about the subject, joined in the writing of the foregoing publication. We hope the information shared in the pages of this book will touch many lives and will influence organisations and society such that the 'lot' of the care-giver becomes a happier one.

Acknowledgements

First, we want to recognise and thank the many UK and US lone parents who participated in the lone-parent study, thus providing direction for the final study. Second, we want to recognise and thank the six participating UK and US organisations, those employees who completed the written survey, the executives who were interviewed and the human resource specialists and officers who championed the study.

Numerous others touched our lives while assisting us with our research, including, but not limited to, some government officials, our families and friends. Space does not permit us to name all of you, but you know who you are.

Finally, we wish to thank our extended and immediate families, Coyne and Lee, who have lived this subject, had less time with us during the journey, but who have been our 'chief supporters' along the way. 'Family comes first' was read over and over again in the survey comments, and we endorse that sentiment fully.

The authors and publisher are grateful to *Human Resource Development International* (2002), Vol. 5: 4, 460–2 (http://www.tandf.co.uk) for permission to reproduce the following figures: 4.1, 4.2, 4.3 and 4.4.

1 Introduction

Caring is the shining thread of gold that holds together the tapestry of life.
Ida V. Moffett, Dean of School of Nursing, Samford University, 1981.

Care-giving responsibilities appear easy to understand. Someone must look after the children and other dependants. French (1993) points out that 'Women have always done it, it is customary.' Certainly, in the corporation culture, women are seen as more committed to family than to career (Schwartz, 1996). Yet, through choice or necessity, not all women stay at home, and, as Rodgers and Rodgers (1989) observed, 'working parents have daily dilemmas: "who will take care of a sick child, who will get the car repaired, who will let the plumber in, who will go to the soccer game and/or attend the school conferences?"' With lone parents, the answer is obvious – that person has the sole responsibility to ensure that care is provided. With married or partnered parents the answer is less obvious, as women increasingly seek to progress in their own careers. For many an employee with serious family responsibilities, the unintended side-effects of the standard work week that is imposed by most employers (UK – 37 hours; USA – 40 hours) has a negative impact upon their career aspirations.

> **Helen** is 46 years old, married, has a high school/secondary education, has children and works part time (20 hours per week) and travels another 4 hours weekly. Her partner works full time. She is part of the clerical staff and earns about 20 per cent of the household income. Helen says that her family commitments have resulted in poor pay and training. She also thinks that her employer neither agrees, understands nor supports her care-giving responsibilities for her children. She is very uncomfortable invoking the care-giving policies and says that 'time off (even for holidays) is becoming a nightmare'. Helen thinks that her career development has been hindered in the past and at present by her care-giving responsibilities.

This book straddles several disparate areas, particularly Human Resource Development (HRD), politics, policy making, women's studies and organisational strategy and governance, to argue that the role of the care-giver is central to the long-term economic and social viability of nations and organisations. We present empirical evidence to show that care-giving is a gender neutral glass ceiling. This fact, teamed with that of a rapidly ageing workforce, calls for urgent attention to be paid to the problem.

Throughout the book we have inserted short vignettes to emphasise our argument. All of these describe real people and situations that we have encountered during the course of our research – only the names have been changed.

Newspapers, business and agenda magazines, scholarly journal articles, non-governmental-organisation publications, legislative committee reports and other such materials are overflowing with 'facts', opinion polls, anecdotal evidence, horror stories, sociological and psychological explanations as to why the 'employment system' is being unfair to mothers, to children, to the care-givers and to the care providers. The majority – childless/'empty-nesters' – have also entered the fray with charges that preference being given to the care-giver employees is at the expense of the childless/empty-nesters.

Joe has been employed 12 years, is a Senior Accountant, with a BSc degree. He is single, 35 years of age, works full time and his mother lives with him. Joe comments: 'It appears that if you are single, the firm thinks you have no other responsibilities and should always be available for them. They don't think us singles have a life outside of the firm.'

All seek to 'change the system' that is seen by some to be oppressive to the carers of our children and elders and by others to be excessively 'coddling' of those who have made the individual choice to be care-givers. At the hub of the employment system are the employers. Many employers are sympathetic to the human drama unfolding around them – at times engulfing them – but all employers must keep a keen eye on their competitive position – locally, nationally and internationally. Governments also have a seat at the table. Not only do democratic governments need to perform their time-honoured task of seeking and leading consensus among the governed but also they must do so within the framework of the unique, never-before-encountered demographic challenges being presented at the dawn of the twenty-first century.

How well society provides for those who cannot provide for themselves is said to be one measure of the term 'civilised' society. Yet how to provide for those who cannot provide for themselves can elicit fierce debate. One culture or nation may see beauty in the State assuming a large measure of primary responsibility for providing for the helpless. Another may see beauty in looking first to the family of the helpless with the State intervening only when it is apparent that that family cannot or will not provide. One firm may see beauty in promulgating 'family-friendly' policies. Another may see beauty in treating all employees alike. One family may see beauty in family self-sufficiency. Another may see beauty in reaching out for community support. All seek the bottom-line solace of knowing that the helpless have found help. Surely the devil is in the details and the debate waxes on not only amongst nations but also, ever more strongly, within organisations and other elements of the nations themselves.

Webster's College Dictionary (1991) defines a care-giver as 'a person who cares for someone who is sick or disabled, or an adult who cares for a child'. Diemut Bubeck (1995) pinpointed the essence: 'care-giving is the kind of work that needs to be done and it is people that are needed to do it [that is, cannot be automated]'. Kossek *et al.* (2001) defined care-giving decisions as the selection of arrangements for the care of a dependant while an individual performs the work role. They claimed that one of the most universal types of non-work decisions that most employees will make during their careers are care-giving decisions.

Throughout the last few millennium – if not always throughout the ages – society has placed a high priority on the care of its children and elders. Society has also placed a high priority on that activity which supports both self and family – work. The pressures and structures of modern living have increased the need for more of the able-bodied citizens to perform remunerative work (usually outside of the home) but have not relieved the need of children and elders to rely on care-givers for their care.

Popenoe (1996) summarised the family that existed at the beginning of the twentieth century by noting that as income-producing work left the home, so too – during the weekday – did the men. Men increasingly withdrew from the direct-care parenting and specialised in the provider or breadwinner role. *The Economist* (July 18–24, 1998) reported that the traditional family model developed in the 1940–60s – a male breadwinner and a mother at home with the children – is not around today for a number of reasons. Single women, either up until marriage or up until the birth of their first child, have always worked. In the past few decades growing numbers of married women are working for pay too. *The Economist* noted that working mothers used to be criticised for neglecting their children; now it is stay-at-home mothers who have to explain themselves. 'Earnings for mothers are not just pin money anymore. For the growing number of single mothers earnings are essential, and in dual-earner families they often make the difference between just getting by and living comfortably.' Catherine Hakim, a feminist academic and senior research fellow in the sociology department at the London School of Economics, as reported by Moore (1996), stated: 'two groups of women have emerged in the past 20 years: career oriented and home-centred'. Hakim, in discussing her 'theory of divided aspirations', maintains that only the career-centred get a hearing from the women's movement. Tom Scarritt (2002), editor of *The Birmingham (Alabama) News*, in an article stressing the need for more women in leadership positions, cautions:

> We must be careful, as we encourage more women to be bank presidents and senators, that we do not discourage those women whose success and fulfilment comes in their roles as wives and mothers, or nurses and teachers, or any other of the vital roles that women have traditionally held. The idea should be to expand the opportunities for our capable daughters, not to direct them or make judgements about the paths they choose.

The home-based society in which women worked to supplement their husbands' income for extras began to recede a generation ago. Now the expectation is that both spouses work. The US labour force now includes more than 70 per cent of all women with children between the ages of 6 and 17 and more than one-half of those women with children less than 1 year old. It is not only a question of who is responsible for very young children – but also, is there anyone home to care for adolescents and the elderly? 'No one intended that the price for business success should be "indifference to family" or that the price of having a family should be to abandon professional ambition' (Rodgers and Rodgers, 1989).

Men also have care-giving responsibilities. More men are obtaining custody of their children in divorce cases now than in the past (15 per cent in the USA and 5 per cent in the UK – with both percentages growing). Kelly (1991) reported that some men, as well as women, opt for changing the definition of success so as to have a greater balance between home and work. Kelly concluded with statistics that showed more men were becoming the primary child-care provider while their wives were working (18 per cent). Schwartz (1992) speculated that because women had not been assimilated fully into business, child-care was not considered a business issue, nor was flexibility thought to be an important company priority. She noted, however, that since women made up a large portion of the nation's workforce, there was no longer a solid family-support structure at home. Only 16 per cent of full-time workers went home to a non-working spouse, according to the US Bureau of Labor Statistics. In two-career couples, neither parent could expect that the other would automatically tend to the needs of their children. Since high-quality affordable day care was rare, many worried parents were permanently anxious about their children (Schwartz, 1992).

Of the many avenues and institutions involved in our lives, the employment relationship is central to providing the sustenance for our dependants and ourselves. The focus of this book is on employees with care-giving responsibilities for dependant children or adults, and the effect, if any, such responsibilities have upon the career development and career progression of employees. This book provides empirical evidence of the effect of one priority (care-giving) upon another (work). The greater the deterrent effect (if any) of care-giving responsibilities upon an employee's career, the lesser will be the employee's earning capacity. Lesser earning capacity translates into lesser ability to provide care for one's self and one's other dependants.

Career progression – like success in any endeavour – requires dedication of time and effort toward that goal. Though many might wish it otherwise, in the market-based economies of the developed world the need for 'committed' employees is seen as the *sine qua non* for long-term economic survival of *any* company – regardless of home country. The pre-

---

Lynn is a 48-year-old single parent with a Masters degree in Business Administration. She is a Vice President of Human Resources. Early in her career she was divorced and assumed responsibility for the care of her two children while working in a male-dominated industry. Lynn's career has spanned nearly 25 years. She recalls that she relied on her family to help with the care of her older child while she was completing her degree and, later, she was very fortunate to find for her younger child a babysitter (the sister of a friend at work) who was flexible and supportive when she had to work long hours. After the divorce the family relocated and the children became 'latch-key' children. They were taught to use the microwave but were not allowed to use the stove to heat their after-school snack. Lynn says she did not have the luxury of getting caught up in the 1980s debate about whether it was better to be at home with your children or to have a fulfilling job.

Lynn now manages the work-life balance programmes and services for the firm and is able to see the evolution in the support that companies provide for working parents. 'When I was raising my children, I did not dare ask to take extra time off after my child's birth. I also did not ask to take time off for doctor's visits.' In order to deal with unexpected child-care needs, Lynn developed a practice of saving her vacation for those emergencies that required her to be away from work. Only in the past few years has she discontinued this practice. Currently, this practice is used mostly by men to spend time with their new-born infant and their families and the phrase 'going undercover' has been coined to describe it. Having complete parenting responsibilities for her two children hampered Lynn's participation in professional organisations and precluded her from taking a more demanding position. When she compares her career progression to that of her peers, she acknowledges that her care-giving responsibilities were a factor in the amount of time it has taken her to achieve her current status. 'Trying to be there for my children and put in the "face-time" (long hours) required to impress the boss also led to my neglecting my personal needs during those years, but I am getting better at taking care of myself everyday,' she says.

vailing concepts and/or perceptions of commitment bring 'time-freedom' to the fore. Time-freedom to pursue a career raises the question 'Is home-base covered?' Is someone else shouldering the care-giving responsibilities of the home so that the employee has the time-freedom to pursue a career? It is a question that faces *any* employee with care-giving responsibilities – regardless of gender.

Our modern reality is that females as well as males have career aspirations and that males as well as females have care-giving responsibilities. However, not all (or even the majority) of employees have care-giving responsibilities. An employer's first duty to the community is to be a profitable, going concern capable of providing, at minimum, sustained employment for existing employees. The empirical evidence reported here provides a key to understanding the underlying conflict between career and family. Whilst career/family conflict may well be considered a reality of long standing, the pressures and structure of modern living have combined to rocket the career/family conundrum into prominence – and public debate.

An underlying theme of this book is provided by the national demographics of the developed world. In the words of Peter Drucker:

> The most important single new certainty – if only because there is no precedent for it in all history – is the collapsing birthrate in the developed world.
>
> (Drucker, 1999)

As firms become squeezed to maintain their competitiveness with an ever-dwindling existing talent base, in their own interest they will need to become more aware of an additional pool of under-utilised talent that is theirs for the asking. Further, declining populations in the Western world have major gross domestic product (GDP) implications for both developed and developing countries. And then there are market growth, production, financial returns, lifestyle effects and more – all of which suggest the potential (if not the certainty) of political responses. The potential of political response begets activists and advocates that cover the full array of opinions – especially in the democracies of the West. Facing the projected increasing scarcity of talent, nations and firms are likely to become increasingly intolerant of the human resource wastage that is the hallmark of today's 'standard' operating practices.

What are the key unanswered questions?

Facts, figures and opinions about aspects of life related to care-giving abound. So much is being written about who is victim and who is victimising – and so little is being subjected to the rigour of primary, empirical research. Basic questions, such as these listed below, cry out for basic answers.

- Does caring for children or elders actually affect ability to have a career?
- Who are being adversely effected? Women? Women and men? Either or both?
- What are the effects of care-giving on the organisation?
- Are there primary causes of any career-adverse effects that apply to all? Are there options available?
- Whose responsibility is it to support care-giving?
- What is fair? And 'fair' to whom?

In all the efforts designed to sway governmental or corporate action one way or the other, many well-thought-out opinions are being offered. Much is supported by secondary research data – a country's Census reports are veritable gold-mines of information – but little firm empirical research has been published. The arguments presented in this book are based on primary data obtained from both care-givers and non-care-givers, male as well as female, in both the UK and the USA.

The multiple roots of care-giving issues add depth and richness – as well as decibels – to the care-giving debates. It seems that each individual issue spawns its own contested area. Straddling the contested areas of care-giving are advocates for women's liberation, individual agency, government policy, social policy, business policy, organisation and national culture. This plethora of viewpoints leads to different ways of investigating the issues. The use of different approaches to the issues begets the use of different methodologies and different results being fed back to different communities and fosters a lack of holism in approach and understanding. HRD, as a discipline that works at the interface between individuals, organisations and policy, lends itself to helping to build a holistic picture and can pull disparate strands together. This empirical investigation of care-giving's effect upon career progression is focused at the interface of academia/public policy/practitioner. We examine a subject matter that by its very nature integrates several fields of research and their associated methodologies. We believe a holistic approach is the best way to capture aspects of the issue that have tradition-ally been overlooked.

Outline of the chapters

The book is divided into three parts. The chapters in the first part bring together the disparate roots and diverse perspectives on the area in order to establish a holistic base in which to locate the empirical evidence. Chapter 2 starts the analysis by locating the area within the literature, and Chapter 3 moves this forward to concentrate the debate on care-giving, looking at the contested area of agency that underlies the care-giving debate – is it the responsibility of the individual, the organisation or the

State? Chapter 4 takes this further, presenting empirical evidence about the gender-free impact of care-giving in the USA and the UK.

The second part presents the main research upon which the views expressed in this book are based. Chapter 5 briefly details the research population and methodology adopted. The following chapters explore different foci arising from the research, namely, the impact that care-giving has upon perceived commitment to work (Chapter 6), upon development opportunities (Chapter 7), upon career attainment (Chapter 8) and for the balance between time available and freedom to pursue a career (time/freedom) (Chapter 9).

Part 3 builds upon the previous two parts by examining the findings in relation to the debates outlined earlier. In particular, Chapter 10 starts this analysis by looking at the importance of the collapsing birth-rate and demographic changes for care-giving practice. The next two chapters of the part examine the tensions engendered by time/freedom for the individual (Chapter 11) and the organisation (Chapter 12). This leads to a discussion in Chapter 13 of policy issues and tensions that arise for the State. Chapter 14 concludes with a discussion and summary of the main points, suggestions for further research and some policy-related remarks.

Part I

Examining the area

This part stands back and looks at the roots of the debates about care-giving and its effect upon career progression. Several academic foci feed into these debates, thus the debates themselves tend to be quite selective in coverage – looking at the area from one perspective or another. Our intention is to develop a more rounded view of the area, in which care-giving and career progression are examined as core issues instead of being brought in on one side or another as incidental aspects of other debates. Through this part, therefore, we seek to establish a holistic base in which to locate the empirical evidence that is presented at the end of this part and in the second part.

Chapter 2 starts the analysis by articulating and briefly reviewing key areas of the literature that have contributed to the development of debates about care-giving and career development – such as the glass ceiling and the domestic labour debate. Chapter 3 builds on these to examine the wider issues that impact upon this area, such as looking at the contested area of agency that underlies the care-giving debate – is care-giving the responsibility of the individual, the organisation or the State? To round off this part, Chapter 4 presents empirical evidence about the gender-free impact of care-giving in the USA and the UK. In doing so it establishes empirically the background to the investigations covered in Part II, as well as providing insight into some of the literature, rhetoric, ideas and opinions explored in the earlier chapters.

2 Diverse perspectives; diverse conclusions

This chapter is devoted to an examination of the diverse perspectives from which the care-giving debate has arisen. Although the intention is not to present a full history of the area, we shall start with a brief overview of the development of the concept and the issues associated with it.

Early perspectives were voiced from within the feminist movement and the domestic labour debate. Although the term 'glass ceiling' was first coined and popularised by the media during the late 1970s, its 'discovery' resulted from the work of the feminist movement over the years.

The feminist movement

The definition of feminism incorporates both a doctrine of equal rights for women (the organised movement to attain women's rights) and an ideology of social transformation aiming to create a world for women beyond simple social equality (Humm, 1992). The first wave of feminism created a new political identity for women and won legal advances and public emancipation for women. It was principally concerned with equalities and 'centres on debates about materialism, about women's individual and collective social and political interests and self-determination'. This wave might be said to have ended around 1949 with the publication of Simone de Beauvoir's *The Second Sex* (Humm, 1992). The second wave of feminism commenced with the politics of reproduction, while sharing with the first wave its politics of legal, educational and economic equal rights for women. 'The core of second wave feminism is reproductive rights' (Humm, 1992). Throughout both waves of feminism is the idea that women are unequal to men because men created the meanings of equality.

One characteristic that distinguishes the feminist movement in Britain from that in America is the British movement's closer ties to the organised Left. Humm pointed out that American second-wave feminism was more marked by liberalism and radicalism, whereas the British Women's Liberation Movement took for granted the long-term socialist traditions of Britain and, in the 1970s, actively engaged with Marxism. The British

Women's Liberation Movement led the debate on the oppression and exploitation of women, which became known as the domestic labour debate.

The domestic labour debate

The 'domestic labour debate' arose in the late 1960s. It was primarily an attempt by the Marxist feminists to provide an account of what they saw as the oppression of women in a capitalist society. The controversy centred around the nature of the relationship between domestic labour and capital accumulation. According to Gardiner (1997), the question had two broad approaches.

> One was to argue that domestic labour subsidised capitalistic produc-
> tion through its role in the reproduction of labour power thus directly
> enhanced profitability. The second approach rejected the notion of
> subsidy but argued instead that domestic labour was essential for the
> reproduction of labour power in capitalist society.

The Marxist feminists' analysis focused on women's unpaid work in their homes, which came to be referred to as 'domestic labour'. Primarily led by their UK adherents, they sought to correct two biases they perceived as being present in the feminist and Marxist literature of the day: first, the focus of various liberal feminists on the allegedly mind-numbing, repetitive, boring and alienating aspects of 'women's work' (the view primarily adopted by US liberal feminists – see *The Feminine Mystique* by Friedan, originally published in 1963); and, second, the almost exclusive focus of Marxist theory on the sphere of production. Marxist feminists sought to correct the first perceived 'error' by focusing on the material aspects of housework and the second by complementing the principles of Marxist theory by focusing on the work performed within the domestic sphere (Bubeck, 1995).

The debate was fierce and the list of criticisms rather long. Perhaps one of Gardiner's conclusions best tells the story: 'The social relations of production in households are different from those of wage labour and need separate investigation' (Gardiner, 1997). Some felt that by putting the debate about housework into a Marxist conceptual framework it became more of an argument among Marxists that a debate within feminism, since most women were excluded by the ideological and academic nature of the argument. The split within the UK and US feminist movements on the most effective approach to the domestic labour debate has caused some to speculate whether the US proponents really understood and/or appreciated the Marxist feminists' theoretical arguments. Perhaps this explanation for the US liberal feminists' lack of support is accurate. It is also possible, however, that the US liberal feminists had a greater understanding of US political arithmetic. Since World War II, no openly avowed Marxist or socialist has ever been elected to national office in the United States. Neither of the two national political parties that have dominated the political discourse of the United States since its inception has ever advocated an anti-capitalist stance. Since action by the State was the ultimate goal of both UK Marxist feminists and US liberal feminists, apparently the US liberal feminists believed that they could more effectively influence the national discourse by emphasising the personal and allegedly demeaning aspects of women's work. 'Feminist economists elsewhere, notably in the USA, engaged more directly with mainstream economics. Although they were still struggling at the fringes of the discipline, they had greater success in establishing a base for their work' (Gardiner, 1997). That they have had some successes is undoubted. That their chosen act has unleashed a forceful 'backlash' is also self-evident. Many, if not most, US women seem to reject the liberal feminist inference that preference/priority for home-related activity somehow equates to disloyalty to their gender. Amongst others, the work of UK feminist Catherine Hakim is noteworthy for its defence of the homemaker. Antonell Picchio (2000) observed: 'what is treated as a woman's issue is in fact a fundamental problem in the system'.

Vivian is 36 years of age, has a high school/secondary school education, is single but is the care-giver for her four school-aged children. She works 28 hours a week with another 1 hour weekly required for travelling to and from work. She earns 100 per cent of the household income as a customer service clerical employee. She states that she has had a mentor in the past and caregiving was never seen to have an impact on her career. In other words, it was never discussed in her performance appraisals. She doesn't think she is maximising her career at present because 'my family are quite young and demanding and I would feel very guilty concentrating on my career'.

Diemut Bubeck (1995) classified 'women's work' into the three categories of housework, child-care and 'caring work', yet the domestic labour debate essentially limited itself to an examination of the housework issues. From a practical viewpoint, it accomplished little and fragmented its proponents into polarised, opposing camps – thus further diminishing their potential for galvanising a consensus for State intervention. However, the debate did spark a broader recognition of women's issues. The debate helped to define women's work and left the door open for the spotlight to shine on the other two (neglected) categories of women's work – child-care and caring work. What the debate did not address was why 'women's' work was indeed women's work. We need to look at the patriarchy debate for this.

The patriarchy debate

In the 1970s and 1980s attempts were made 'to apply "exploitation" to men's appropriation of female domestic labour and to develop an analysis of patriarchy to complement Marxist analysis of capitalism' (Gardiner, 1997). Patriarchy – 'rule by the father' – has a long tradition. In seventeenth-century England, patriarchy was the dominant political philosophy. The king, as father of his people, had absolute authority over his subjects; fathers had natural authority over their wives and children. The 'rule by fathers' concept was used by Marx and Engels in an economic (rather than political) dimension. They identified the pre-capitalist phase of history, when families/households were property owning and producing units as the patriarchal mode since the ownership and direction of the production process was vested in male/paternal heads of household. Women as wives held economic value both for their actual labour contribution and for their ability to reproduce. Husbands needed to control the reproduction ability of their wives for two reasons: first, because large numbers of children were needed both for labour itself and to ensure that some would survive to perpetuate the family workforce; and, second, because the husbands wished to ensure that they themselves were the fathers of their heirs (Gardiner, 1997).

Radical feminists in the late 1970s began using patriarchy as a term for referring to men's power over women in a more general way – one well removed from that of the rule of the father. 'Within radical feminist theory, patriarchy was no longer confined to analysing power relations within the family or at an interpersonal level but began to be applied to the relations between men and women throughout all of society's institutions' (Gardiner, 1997). Humm defined patriarchy more simply: 'A system of male authority which oppresses women through its social, political and economic institutions' (Humm, 1992).

Theorising on women's oppression in general became the focus of the debate, rather than the debate being limited to the domestic labour issue. Therefore, the patriarchy debate had both a broader agenda and a broader social science base than did the domestic labour debate. More specific studies were undertaken, such as studies of patriarchy and work focused on gender relations in employment. Feminist interests began to shift away from economics towards sociology and anthropology (Gardiner, 1997). The term 'patriarchy' was used for extending the debate beyond the liberal feminist emphasis on the ideology of sexism and into the broader arena for extending the understanding of gender inequality. With broader appeal, it became important as a political concept that signalled the struggle against the nature and totality of oppressive and exploitative relations affecting women (Mies, 1986; Gardiner, 1997). In summarising the different feminist attempts to apply exploitation to gender relations, Gardiner concluded that the exploitation concept was both unnecessary and unhelpful from an analytical standpoint. She pointed out that the concept of exploitation was not needed to be able to demonstrate gender inequality and felt it was more productive to concentrate on collecting and analysing the more straightforward empirical data relating to time use, income, and consumption patterns. She concluded:

> Another reason for rejecting exploitation as a useful concept for analysing domestic labour is the way it diverts attention away from what has become the central component of domestic labour in industrial capitalist societies, namely the care of dependant children and adults.
>
> (Gardiner, 1997)

Discrimination debates and the 'glass ceiling'

Webster's College Dictionary (1991) defined the glass ceiling as 'an upper limit to professional advancement, especially as imposed upon women, that is not readily perceived or openly acknowledged'. 'The term "glass ceiling" has been widely accepted as a metaphor to explain the paucity of women in upper management' (McQuarrie, 1994). Hasslette, Geis and Carter (1992) defined the glass ceiling as 'the exclusion of women from higher status positions'. 'The [glass] ceiling is a cap beyond which women find it difficult to break into higher level positions because of sociological restrictions which have the effect of limiting their opportunities for career development' (Kleiman, 1996). 'The glass ceiling is a barrier to the advancement to the higher levels of the organisation' (Noe, Hollenbeck, Gerhart and Wright 1997). For the purposes of this work, the definition as provided by *Webster's College Dictionary* is adopted. Webster's definition emphasises that the glass ceiling is an upper limit to professional advancement that is not readily perceived or openly acknowledged. Although noting that the glass ceiling is especially imposed upon women, it does not limit the term solely to women and expressly defines it as a limitation on professional advancement for reasons that are either not readily perceived or not openly acknowledged. Adoption of this definition of the glass ceiling allows, and in fact encourages, the search for limitations to professional advancement – wherever they may be.

A number of possible explanations for the paucity of women in senior-level executive positions have been offered for the glass ceiling phenomenon. The literature points to four main areas of investigation, namely: job discrimination; perceptions of personal achievement; the role of in-house training and development; and home-based issues such as care-giving. The first two areas could be squared with notions of objective and subjective aspects of career development in which job discrimination explains existing and structural differences between the career paths of men and women (and, if we were to widen the debate further, around class, race and so on), whilst the perception of personal career development points to individually driven aspects of career development such as aspirations and belief that one has, or has not, been discriminated against. The latter two areas are both concerned with the opportunities available for an individual's career development and what might influence them. In-house provision addresses the role of the employer in supporting an individual's career development, whilst care-giving articulates the role of some of the factors external to the work situation that might impact upon the individual's ability to make use of whatever opportunities are offered. These four strands are not mutually exclusive, but their effects intersect with and influence each other. However, each of these is introduced briefly here and is addressed more fully in the introduction of empirical evidence in Part 2. Each area is not discrete, and whilst the discussion here attempts to pull the different areas apart, it can be seen, even in the early stages of the book, that there is a great need for empirical evidence (such as that presented in Part 2) that examines them in a more comparable fashion.

Job discrimination

Differential rates of pay can be seen as an indicator of discrimination. Felice Schwartz (1992) maintained that at the time of her research approximately 37 per cent of the managers in US business were women, and Jackson (2000) found that in 1994, 8.9 per cent of corporate officers in the USA were women, whereas in 1995 10.1 per cent were women. However, most of these women were in jobs at the bottom of the team's pyramid. Korenman and Neumark (1991), Loh (1996) and Gray (1997) have all found that married men earn higher wages than unmarried men even when education and work experience are controlled. Studies investigating the effects of marriage on women's earnings have been less conclusive. Studies based on recent data (Blau and Beller, 1988; Waldfogel, 1997) found that married women also enjoyed an earnings advantage. Chandler, Kamo and Werbel (1994), citing data from the National Survey of Families and Households, conclude that delaying marriage significantly increases married women's wages and does not significantly affect married men's wages, but that delaying childbirth significantly increases both married women's and married men's wages.

In Britain there is evidence of increasing polarisation in the job market between part-time employees – both women and men – and full-time employees – both women and men. Coyle (1996) reported that in the 1970s, part-time employees earned 80 per cent of the pay of full-timers, but by the 1990s this had dropped to 72 per cent. She felt that the gender gap had been overtaken by the status gap. In one longitudinal study, men had a 36 per cent pay lead on full-time women in 1978 whilst full-time women had a 40 per cent pay lead on part-time women. By the mid 1990s the lead of men over full-time women employees had shrunk to 20 per cent, but the spread between full-time and part-time female employees had grown to 52 per cent.

Job content has also been seen to be a factor in job discrimination. As reported by McQuarrie (1994), the Ohlott, Ruderman and McCauley report showed that male managers' jobs included different developmental challenges than female managers. Male managers performed tasks with higher levels of visibility and clearer deadlines, held jobs with larger scope and greater responsibilities for managing multiple functions and worked at jobs characterised by external pressures. However, men and women did not differ in the number of other developmental components in their jobs, and women did not encounter different obstacles than men. The authors of the report argue that whilst the differences in job content were relatively slight, they were significant because they represented subtle forms of discrimination in the career paths of women and men that otherwise were difficult to discern on the surface. Many men admitted to making the assumption that women would not want the travelling and extra work linked to 'trophy' assignments (Flynn, 1996). Parallel with this, a study by Catalyst (a leading US non-profit organisation working to advance women in business) showed that male CEOs said that the chief factor to hold back women's advancement was their 'lack of significant general management or line experience'. Women ranked this factor third (Associated Press, February 28, 1996, 3D). Women may miss out on key assignments and the opportunity to demonstrate their competency because they are assigned tasks with less responsibility than men. And, if women receive 'less personal support', they may experience more stress, which may translate into greater turnover for women in middle management ranks (McQuarrie, 1994). There was a female consensus that working long hours and exceeding performance standards were what it took to crack the glass ceiling (Leonard, 1996).

Zelda is a care-giver with one small infant and one kindergarten-age child. She is married with a full-time working partner. She has a high school/secondary school education and earns 50 per cent of the household income. She works 22 hours per week and travels an additional 8 hours per week to and from work. Zelda took a demotion after the birth of her children and accepted part-time work. She strongly disagrees that her employer understands and supports her child-care efforts. Zelda had this to say: 'I have been unable to work long hours because I have chosen to work reduced hours. In a previous role, my head of department said, "why should I choose you above someone who can work full time?" Some managers still equate promotion with someone who works full time and long hours.'

Perceptions of personal achievement

The idea that women can be disadvantaged in terms of being awarded the 'plum' jobs leads us to the next area identified as a factor of the glass ceiling, namely that of perceptions of personal achievement or career attainment. A field study by Tsui and Gutek (1984) investigated gender differences in performance and evaluated the success of male and female managers. The sample consisted of 217 male and 78 female middle-level managers in a multi-company corporation. The female managers in the sample on average were younger, had less company tenure and less management experience than the male managers. Six survey questionnaires were sent to each participant – one for the subject's self-report, two for peers, two for subordinates and one for a superior of the subject. On average, women received higher performance ratings than men. Female managers enjoyed larger merit increases and faster promotions, as well as higher levels of job satisfaction than male managers. However, women worked at lower grade levels than men. A follow-up study with the same subjects 18 months after the initial study failed to provide further evidence of pro-male bias in middle-management of the studied corporation (Tsui and Gutek, 1984).

Catalyst reports a Seagram Company sponsored survey of women with top-level jobs that found that only 5 per cent of senior management positions at Fortune 500 companies were held by women. Male stereotyping was reported as the top stumbling block by 52 per cent of the females responding to the survey. Less than 25 per cent of the males cited male stereotyping as a serious problem. Eighty per cent of the male CEOs surveyed reported lack of experience as the prime obstacle preventing women from advancing, and 45 per cent of the women executives agreed. 'International experience is given almost as much weight as operations these days' (Dunkel, 1996). Brooks Jackson (2000) made the point that the mathematical averaging of the US Census Bureau graphs shows that females make only US$0.73 for every US$1.00 of male earnings because it does not compare men and women of equal experience. In the USA, women have an average of four and a half fewer years on the job.

The picture is much starker, however, when we look at gendered perceptions of career aspiration rather than just the achievement figures. Hill (1993) said that the most frequently debated topic in legal cases involving gender discrimination 'revolves around the issue of interest of women in non-traditional, higher-paying jobs'. She stated that Mary Joe Frug, in her book *Women and the Law*, showed that conservative courts have ruled that women as a group display job preferences different from men and are less interested in the more competitive job positions that yield higher rewards. In *US Equal Employment Opportunity Commission (EEOC)* v. *Sears*, it was alleged that Sears had engaged in sex discrimination in hiring and promoting men into commission sales jobs and relegating women to much lower-paying, non-commission sales jobs. The judge threw out the EEOC's statistical analyses as 'meaningless' because they were based on the faulty assumption that female sales applicants were as interested as male applicants in commission sales jobs. 'Basically,' said the judge, 'women are "feminine", non-traditional work is "masculine", and therefore women do not want to do it.'

The US courts are not alone in reinforcing 'traditional' role concepts. In 2002, the (UK) Court of Appeal upheld the principle that children should be brought up by their mothers rather than their fathers when it rejected a custody claim by a stay-at-home dad. The father claimed sexual discrimination in the original custody award as he had brought up the children while his wife pursued a well-paid career. However, the Lord Justice stated that in spite of the 'unusual role reversal', he could not 'ignore the realities involving the different roles and functions of men and women' (HomeDad.org.uk, Tuesday 21 May 2002).

In-house training and development

These perceptions can influence the extent to which training and development is made available to women, which is the third main area identified as contributing to the glass ceiling. Training and development is a key ingredient in fostering and catalysing the sort of experience found to be lacking in women by those such as the CEO's cited above. Training is obviously expensive for the firm. The cost of losing a typical worker has been stated as US$50,000 (Reingold, 1999). Others stress that the cost of turnover is related to the salary of the departing worker with most using a percentage of annual income. 150 per cent of the departing employee's salary appears to be one of the more popular estimates (Fandray, 2000).

This can be seen through the lens of human capital theory, in which 'human capital' referred to 'the knowledge workers acquired through the investment of time and money to become more productive' (Cohn, 1996). Human capital theory paralleled the neoclassical theory of wages by arguing that wages were tied to productivity. However, unlike orthodox neoclassicism, human capital theory argued that wages were not determined by productivity alone, but also by the cash returns to workers who had invested in increasing their work-related skills. Hasslette, Geis and Carter (1992) described human capital theory as a theory of earnings as returns on investment in job training and experience. They also reminded us that economists had been using the theory to explain salary differences between men and women. They listed the factors studied as years of education, years of work experience, job interruptions, part-time work, job area and industry, and job level (for example, line versus staff), marriage and children, family background, and personality traits. They concluded that there were fewer women managers in production and engineering, metals and investment banking – all areas with higher managerial salaries

– and that women were less likely to hold line positions, which were associated with better promotion prospects. Further, they claimed that marriage and children decreased women's salaries and pointed to the decreased geographic mobility resulting from parenthood as a partial explanation.

From this perspective, organisations need to balance the cost of training against the anticipated financial benefit to be accrued from the development of the person. Cohn (1996) suggests that women are more likely than men to quit their jobs prematurely, thus, in accordance with human capital theory, 'firms are reluctant to hire them for positions that involve employer-financed training . . . jobs that involve high levels of firm-specific skills'. Diane Coyle (1996) noted that the improving educational standards of women provides part of the explanation of the narrowing of the pay gap between women and men, but she comments 'Not very much, though – after all, full-time women are now better qualified on the average than full-time men but still get paid less' (Coyle, 1996). In contrast, however, *The UK Employment Gazette* (April 1994) reported that the Labour Force Survey data on training in the previous four weeks showed that very similar proportions of male and female employees of working age experienced job-related training (13.5 per cent of male employees and 14.5 per cent of female employees in Autumn 1993). One of the complications in examining this area is the wide range of what might be included in or meant by particular forms of training. If we throw the net wider to include more informal forms of training and development, is the picture the same?

Flynn (1966) reports that there was a lack of mentoring and networking opportunities available to women. Yet the importance of mentoring and support is well documented. Armstrong (1995) and Hill (1993), in listing some key determinants of successful careers for women, gave prominent attention to 'presence of mentors and sponsors throughout career'. Hill (1993) cites mentoring as one of the prevalent reasons for career growth. Two reasons for the lack of the universality of informal

---

Shelia is in her early thirties, with a BSc degree, has been with the firm for 10 years and works currently as a Human Resource Generalist. She progressed through the Management Trainee ranks. In her current position she supervises two recruiters and the bank internship employees during the summer months. She has a mentor. Shelia works full time, is single and does not have dependants. She sees care-giving policies and practices as being very good for her company and has seen no negative impact arising from these policies in her career. Shelia said: 'The firm is very family friendly so I can still have a rewarding career after marriage and a family. That is a real plus for young women coming in who want to have it all – a career and children.'

mentoring were advanced by Long (1990): first, men are sometimes reluctant to mentor women because of fears about the connotations of the relationship; and, second, questions exist about career commitment among women with children.

It is worth noting that examining the utility of training through the financial balance of inputs and outputs is dangerously restrictive (as well as hard to measure) as there is evidence that training and development also have a retention value. Reingold (1999) reported that a study by Emerging Workforce in 1999 showed that 35 per cent of employees who don't receive regular mentoring plan to look for another job within 12 months whilst only 16 per cent of those with good mentors expect to jump ship. Similarly, 41 per cent of those who said their company offered poor training planned to leave within a year, while only 12 per cent of those who rated training opportunities as excellent planned to leave.

Home-based issues

The fourth aspect of the glass ceiling was identified as relating to home-based issues. This area is the focus of the book, but cannot be taken in isolation from the other three areas. The main focus of the literature in this area has been upon the woman's role in raising a family. Little attention has been paid to the need for care-giving to elder dependants (and others) or to the male role in this area.

Hill (1993) said Frug stated that since 1967, the 'lack of interest' argument has been used widely to justify patterns of sex segregation in corporate worlds. Jones and Causer (1995) argue that

> organisation policies and practices in respect of this group continue to be underpinned by the 'norm' of the typical male employee whose family commitments impinge marginally, if at all, on work responsibilities. Women, as actual or potential mothers, continue to be seen as deviants from this norm, whose family commitments are likely to adversely affect work performance or commitment.

The authors state that numerous studies have identified both potential motherhood and motherhood as 'impacting detrimentally' on women's opportunities for employment and promotion. Traditionally the solution rested with the individual in the form of choosing to leave employment for a 'greater or lesser' period.

For this reason, part-time work has normally been associated with female care-givers. Davidson and Cooper (1993) asserted that the growth of part-time work may also have played a part in the increase in the number of women with second jobs in the European Community; this more than doubled between 1983 and 1988. This increase suggested that women wanted – or needed – to work more hours. Part-time work, however, is traditionally not rewarded in the same manner as full-time work nor does it have the same status.

Treanor (2001) reports the view of the Confederation of British Industries (CBI) that the main causes of pay differences between males and females are the large number of women working in low-paid sectors and the many women taking career breaks or working part-time because of child-care responsibilities. 'Fewer hours bring lesser rewards. Though the underlying trend is for women's rates of pay increasingly to match those of men, when hourly rates are compared, women in the UK average 78% of the men's rate.' Catherine Hakim (1996) maintained that pay-gap issues were 'completely explained by differences in occupational grade and promotion within occupations'. She said that there was some sex discrimination, but there was a 'statistical distortion'. 'If more women applied for senior positions, the proportion claimed to be victims would statistically fall.' She also said that most men and women still regard wives as having primary responsibility for housework and husbands as having the main responsibility for breadwinning. 'Across Europe, the modern sexual division of labour, which allows the wife to work as a secondary earner, often part-time, has replaced separate roles,' said Hakim. 'Only among the young is there acceptance of equal, parallel roles in marriage' (Moore, 1996).

Thomas is 35 years of age and works as a Senior Staff Engineer in the IT Department. Employed for 12 years, Thomas normally works 42 hours per week and travels an additional 5 hours weekly to and from work. Special projects and assignments result in additional hours for him. He is married, with his partner working part time. She earns 30 per cent of the household income. They have three small children. Currently, they share most of the child-care responsibilities. He has this to say: 'The way my career is developing (fast-paced with more overtime), it may be difficult in the future to share in any child-care for my children. This could involve my partner having to give up work to do all the child-care, resulting in a loss of earnings to our household.'

Jones and Causer (1995) report that in the late 1980s organisations began to devise measures to attract and retain female employees because of skill shortages in the workforce. They assert that the motivation behind these measures was the 'cost of training rather than an intrinsic interest in the benefits to women'. Some companies with high proportions of female staff developed career-break schemes and enhanced maternity-leave packages. They also 'began to explore the feasibility of alternative patterns of work within the organization as a means of reducing the high turnover rates amongst female professionals with families'. However, Amy Techner of Evanston, Illinois, may have spoken for many when she said 'Maybe it can work when things are booming ... but not now'. After a 20-year marketing career, this mother of two concluded that in good times pay raises and stock options made it tough to walk away, 'But in a downturn, it's a little tougher to convince yourself that the trade-offs are worth it. It's simply easier to leave' (Rubin, 2003).

Cracks in the glass ceiling?

The brief overview of debates around the glass ceiling indicates the complexity and ubiquity of the area. However, the *Wilson Quarterly* (2002) reports the Marianne Bertrand and Kevin Hallock study that shows more cracks in the corporate 'glass ceiling' than most social commentators have noticed. In a statistical analysis of 1,500 companies the pair concludes that pay equity is now pretty well established. Noting that in 1992 only 5.4 per cent of firms had women in their top five executive positions and by 1997 the percentage had risen to 15 per cent, and reporting that the average female in the study received US$900,000 per year while the men pocketed US$1,300,000, they note that the gap isn't quite what it appears to be. Bertrand and Hallock felt the difference was explained by several factors, most notably that women were underrepresented in the biggest corporations that offer the biggest pay packets, and that the women in the study were on average five years younger in age than the men. Overall, they reported that the unexplained gender compensation gap for top executives was less than 5 per cent. Irene Bruegel (2000) maintains that in Britain women are earning about one-third of household income, a proportion about 50 per cent higher than in the early 1970s. She attributes this partly to high male unemployment and early male retirement from the workforce, but also notes that the trend arises from the long-term improvement in the educational achievements and aspirations of young women. She maintains that this improvement reflects new opportunities for women, the spread of feminist consciousness and the growing recognition that marriage can no longer secure a woman's economic welfare.

Similarly, although the arguments of the glass ceiling are generally focused upon the female, and thus the female role, there is some evidence that some men are also disadvantaged. The shift from the traditional pattern of male breadwinner and female housekeeper also impacts upon the (non-traditional) father in a dual-earner household. Barrett (1995) reported a study of twenty Fortune 500 companies. She said this study showed 'that fathers from dual-earner households may be victims of salary discrimination in the same way women have been discriminated against as a group'. A wage gap of 11 per cent in salary increases existed between traditional fathers and fathers in dual-earner households when compared in terms of education, tenure, job commitment and family values.

Over the 5-year period salary increases were 70 per cent for the traditional father and only 59 per cent for the dual-earner father. The gap may be a matter of corporate prejudice in addition to objective factors. Fifty-three hours worked for traditional fathers per week versus 51 hours for fathers from dual-earner families account for some of the gap, but the authors could not rule out the traditional non-employed 'wife as a resource' explanation for the salary gap. The authors suggested a 'double negative economic impact on these families'.

In summary, this chapter has provided a brief overview of the threads that contribute to the debate but has suggested that these threads are tightly woven, if not knotted! There are a lot of statistics around, and many interpretations; however, many of these are not directly comparable. In addition, as indicated above, the role of the care-giver, whilst included in much of the literature, is normally discussed as an adjunct to the main argument of the piece. In the next chapter this role is given centre stage.

3   Broadening the debate

The previous chapter outlined some of the debates and statistics surrounding discussions of the glass ceiling, which generally place the role of the care-giver to the side of the main debate. In addition, where care-giving is covered, it is normally focused exclusively on care for children, and is seen as a female prerogative. In this chapter care-giving, in the wider sense, is brought into the centre of the discussion.

Eric has a BSc degree, 14 years' service and is a senior manager/officer with the firm. He works full time, is in his mid thirties, is married and has two children. His partner also works full time. They share the child-care responsibilities. They have a child-minder to assist at home. When asked about the work/life issues, Eric shared his opinions: 'Having watched the expectation of "hours" people put in to rise over 10 years, I have been sur-prised that it hasn't caused more complaints than it has. Obviously people are very committed to their jobs, sometimes more than they should be. Some people don't get the balance and they suffer, but it doesn't show externally. I am determined not to neglect my children and not to miss out on their growing up because of work. Sure work is very important, but you have to strike a balance in your life. It's a good thing – a large portion of our staff are women – that affects the culture of the firm – even nowadays women tend to be primary care-givers with children and family. I think with more women in management, this will have a bearing on how the firm deals with it.'

A brief chronology of care-giving and the division of labour

In the evolutionary leap to *Homo sapiens*, the traditional view is that the men of the clan provided food by hunting whilst the women stayed around the cave minding the children. Thus, in conventional theory, males were primarily responsible for the leap to *Homo sapiens*. This view is not without its doubters. Kristen Hawes, an anthropologist at the University of Utah, puts forth that grandmothers were crucial in the genus *Homo* evolution to its present state (Boyd, 2003). Her 'grandmothering hypothesis' describes how grandmothers, with no young children of their own, helped feed their daughters' offspring in tribes too primitive to practise agriculture. She reasons that men in those tribes hunt game but that game hunting was an inefficient method of feeding their families, compared with the women's work of gathering and preparing berries, edible roots and fruits. Fast-forwarding to the more well-known 'farm days', nearly everybody worked in the fields – children included. 'Home' was located in or near the fields and the labour of all was needed for the good of the whole. Males generally undertook the hard, physical labour requiring brute strength for extended hours. Females also did hard labour in the fields, interspersed, with time allotted for meal preparation and other 'home' chores.

Gender-based division of care-giving responsibilities has probably always been present to some degree – mother nurtures, father disciplines, and so on – yet the arrangement was informal and changed as circumstances and personal preferences dictated. 'Marriage in the pre-industrial family was primarily an economic arrangement, not the strongly emotional connection based on the romantic that it was later to become; the purpose of marriage was economic survival in tough times' (Popenoe, 1996). The father as the designated head of the pre-modern European family and household was a powerful figure. Father power rested on ownership of land, the primary basis of production.

The modern nuclear family began in north-western Europe a few centuries before the Industrial Revolution of the late 1700s. As the economy expanded beyond its agricultural base, the venue of production shifted from the fields to the factories. People followed the better-paying jobs, which were remote from their homes. Thus, the care-giving issue was moved to 'the front burner'. Informal arrangement for gender-based division of care-giving responsibilities no longer fitted the times. Along with the industrial economy and its locus of production being removed from the immediate area of the home came the first true care-giving conundrum: who should work at the remote location and who should look after the home and the children?

As industrial society grew rapidly, so did abuses of 'the system'. Child-labour laws and subsequently the mandatory child-education laws reduced much of the conscience-offending abuses yet had the possibly unintended effect of crystallising the care-giving issue within the family. The introduction of the 'family' or 'living wage' and, eventually, the protective legislation produced a new blueprint, that of the breadwinner/homemaker model with a gendered separation of spheres into paid and domestic work (Glickman, 1997). This model became the cultural template, the default arrangement for American life in the middle of the twentieth century (Moen and Yu, 2000). As children can only be at home or at school – not at work – someone must 'stay behind' and care for them when they are at home. Generally, the gender division of duties that became embedded into the expectations of society was that, where possible, males should assume the breadwinner role and females the care-giver role.

Tracey Warren, Karen Rowlingson and Claire Whyley (2001) chart the typical male pattern of work history as a continuous and full-time labour-market attachment whilst the female pattern is reduced and made discontinuous by women's caring for children and other dependants. They maintain that the result of this pattern is that women have fewer years in which to move up the wage hierarchies, and they have also tended to face downward mobility into lower paying jobs after taking time out from employment. They note, however, that the younger cohorts of women are moving closer to the continuous full-time labour market attachment pattern of men and are taking less time out of the labour market for child-bearing.

Today our economy needs the most skilled and productive workforce it can find in order to remain competitive. The same workforce must reproduce itself and give adequate care to the children who will be the future workforce. Workers with children, especially women, often find themselves at a serious disadvantage in the workplace. Among Western democracies, the USA ranks third, behind Scandinavia and Canada, in its dependence on women in the workforce. Yesteryear's exception to the norm was that both parents worked. Today, that exception has become the norm.

Fuchs (1989) states: 'In contemporary America, the greatest barrier to economic equality is children. Since most women want to bear children and are concerned about their well-being once they are born, the "propensity to mother" puts women at a disadvantage.' Felice Schwartz (1989) found that the majority of women 'want to pursue serious careers while participating actively in the rearing of children'. She also suggested that most of them are willing to trade some career growth and compensation for freedom from the constant pressure to work long hours and weekends. However, Kate Lauderbaugh, former bank executive, concluded that management and motherhood were incompatible. She is now home with her two children – ages 14 months and 4 years old – and sums up the ambivalence: 'Its been really good for my kids, but I'm not sure it's been great for me' (Rubin, 2003).

By the latter half of the 1990s, there appeared to be a declining emphasis on the allegations of career discrimination against females and a broadening of the emphasis to identify more specifically the ramifications of some of these self-imposed responsibilities that were adversely affecting career development. This lessening of the focus on discrimination against females could possibly have been due to: (1) success of the advocates demanding elimination of discrimination; (2) rejection by many females of the perceived charge that females with non-career aspirations were letting the side down – backlash; (3) self-admission that total commitment to company success was beyond the capability or desire of many of those having private commitments to other priorities that they valued more highly than career; (4) dramatic drop in the unemployment rate (or dramatic increase in employment levels), which placed a premium on finding and developing talent – wherever that talent might be; (5) combinations of the foregoing or other less obvious reasons. The broadening of the emphasis to identify more specifically the ramifications of self-imposed responsibilities that potentially affect career development brings the subject of care-giving to the fore.

Beth, Senior Management Executive, has a mentor as well as a BSc degree. She is 39 years of age and has one child in grammar school. Her partner works full time. Beth works part time, 31 hours a week, and incurs 5 hours' a week travel to and from work. Beth is able to accept most extra assignments without notice and all extra required assignments with notice. Beth does have some child-care issues even though she feels her supervisor at work is very flexible with her working arrangements. Beth has this to say: 'I am capable of more responsibility, but I do not have (or want to give) more time to work.'

Some examples of work/life initiatives

Before moving away from an examination of the historical development of care-giving it is worth noting that there are now many initiatives in place to help employees balance the tensions between work and home. Some are specifically related to support for child-care, but not all. We outline some of the more common ones.

Child-care assistance

This takes many forms from child-care referral services to providing on-site day-care centres. A 1995 survey of 1,050 companies reports that 85 per cent of surveyed companies provided some type of child-care assistance. There are anecdotal reports from some companies that credit such programmes with reducing absenteeism. Some point to on-site day care as increasing employee control over their work and non-work schedules, which makes it easier for them to manage the daily demands of work and family life. However, Goff *et al.* (1990) found there was very little benefit to employers providing on-site care in areas in which quality day care is already available. And there remains the uncertain non-care-giver reaction to such use of corporate benefit dollars.

Compressed work week (usually four 10-hour days)

In addition to giving employees an open day in the week for taking care of personal matters, including family demands, and conveying a sense of increasing control and decreasing work/family strain, some research claims positive effects on somatic health complaints (for example, headaches, insomnia). However, other research has shown that compressed work weeks can result in fatigue for employees as well as additional stress on supervisors due to the longer work day (Sherman *et al.*, 1998).

Flextime (allowing employees flexible schedules for beginning and ending work)

According to Golden (1997), 27 per cent of full-time wage and salary workers in the USA had these options in May 1997, up from the Bureau of Labor Statistics report of 15.1 per cent in May 1991. This benefit is reported as reducing traditional sources of absenteeism and tardiness and is associated with greater job satisfaction and a lessening of work/family pressures. On the downside, it is not appropriate for some jobs, can cause communications problems and may force managers to extend working hours to cover various schedules (Sherman *et al.*, 1998).

Job sharing

This has many of the same benefits as flextime and is another way to reduce work/family conflict. Recent, limited research covering sixty-nine pairs of job sharers reports that 90 per cent were adjudged to be performing at a higher level than comparable full-time employees in the same job, with 30 per cent perceived to have a 30 per cent increase in output when compared to one person doing the same job. However, job sharing requires organisations to hire and train two people for one job; also, greater benefits and salary costs are often associated with job sharing.

Telecommunicating (allows worker to work from home and can ease child-care and elder-care responsibilities)

The Bureau of Labour Statistics (1998) reports that more than 21 million persons did some work from home as part of their primary job in 1997. Higher productivity and job satisfaction have been reported. However, additional technology/equipment costs, limited communications and less control over employees can be disadvantages.

Each of these initiatives (amongst many others) is designed to help employees and organisations balance the tensions between home and work. These tensions are explored more fully in Part 3.

Care-giving as a fundamental career constraint

Care-giving is just one of the work/life tensions that these initiatives are designed to support – however, it is a major issue for many. Intertwined amongst the positions of the protagonists on either side of the glass ceiling debate is the notion of care-giving – care of children; care of elders.

> In many of the European Union countries there is a great concern about the provision of childcare facilities, which are felt to be a pre-requisite to encourage women to enter either the world of business or corporate life. Particularly, in the UK, there is emphasis on the need for a widespread and professional service, as well as the infrastructure to enable women to financially avail themselves of the facilities.
>
> (Davidson and Cooper, 1993)

Numerous studies have identified both potential motherhood and the reality of motherhood as 'impacting detrimentally on women's opportunity for employment and promotion' (Jones and Causer, 1995).

In addition, there is growing evidence that workers are putting in more hours on the job than was the case in the middle of the twentieth century (Clarksberg and Moen, 2000) – or at least are experiencing the feelings of being rushed and overworked (Robinson and Godbey, 1997). The culture in organisations tends to equate time spent on the job with being success-ful at work (Hochchild, 1997), however, work remains structured for the most part in the mid-twentieth-century mould of 'breadwinner/ homemaker' model, that is non-recognition of family responsibilities or other non-work-related personal involvements. Similarly, Moen and Yu (2000) comment that the organisation of paid work – and the culture spawned by paid work – remains largely unchanged from the past. With the path of men's life largely unchanged, they maintain that it is the women who have had to accommodate the structural lag produced by the changing realities of the work/family interface. Furthermore, many adults, mostly women, also care for ageing parents whilst continuing to provide substantial support for their children. One US government study of family care-givers found that 23 per cent of working women had to reduce working hours, 35 per cent rearranged their schedules and 25 per cent took time off without pay to care for elderly parents (Hordern, 1996). In addition, the stresses being experienced by workers in two-earner families are often viewed as 'private troubles' rather than gendered and 'public' issues.

Moen and Yu maintain that families have always devised various strat-egies to deal with the inevitable exigencies that occur in life. They point out that during times of major upheaval, when old rules and routines no longer apply, individual households may adopt various lines of adaptation and that eventually new blueprints for living become part of the institutional landscape. However, they emphasise that during this process there is inevitably a period of structural lag. They maintain that the entrance of women of all ages into the labour force in the second half of the twentieth century has created another period of structural lag. Contemporary institutions remain predicated on the breadwinner/homemaker model in spite of the fact that increasingly fewer workers (male or female) have family members at home to manage the non-work aspects of their lives and to facilitate their success at work.

Debra, 39 years of age, with a high school/secondary school education, is married. Both she and her partner work full time. She provides 35 per cent of the household income and works 40 hours per week, with travel time consuming another 1 hour per day. She has one child and works as a Mortgage Service Assistant. Because of her child-care requirements, she is not able to accept any assignments outside of her normal scheduled hours. Debra had this to say: 'Due to commitments with my family, I have not gone for promotion to be able to provide my employer with longer working hours.'

Work continues in the field for determining modern-day coping strategies for the career constraint of care-giving. Writing in the *Journal of Marriage and the Family*, Becker and Moen (1999) reported the results of in-depth interviews with 100 people in middle-class dual-earner couples in upstate New York to investigate the range of couples' work–family strategies. They found that the majority were not pursuing two high-powered careers but were typically engaged in what they termed 'scaling-back' strategies. They identified three scaling-back strategies as: placing limits (usually on the number of hours of work that the couple would undertake); having a one-job, one-career family; or 'trading off' (a combination of the other two strategies, which could alter over the couple's life course).

Care-givers in the workforce: UK demographics

Browne (1998) reports Julian Steer of the Centre for Economic Performance at the London School of Economics, one of the authors of a book called *The State of Working Britain*, as stating: 'Almost half the women in the UK with a child under 12 months are working, as are two-thirds of those with children under age ten.' In 1981, fewer than one in five women with babies under the age of 1 year were working. Half of those with children under the age of 10 had jobs. The main reason for change is the wider provision of maternity rights, according to Steer. In the UK national maternity leave legislation was passed in 1978, extended in 1993 and extended further in 2003 to entitle all women with two years' employment by the same company to 26 weeks of paid leave and an additional 26 weeks of unpaid leave. Evidence from many countries shows that maternity-leave coverage has a strong effect on women's job retention after giving birth. Julian Steer, quoted by Browne (1998), says: 'These developments have allowed women to build a career and invest in human capital thereby raising the probability of securing employment after childbirth.' Almost all the increase in employment is among those with working partners (Browne, 1998). However, Davidson and Cooper caution: 'In the U.K., the barriers to equality for women are general and pervasive and include: out-moded attitudes about the role of women; direct and indirect discrimination; the absence of proper childcare provision; and inflexible structures for work and careers' (Davidson and Cooper, 1993).

Labour Market Trends, November 2000 (UK Office of National Statistics) listed the number of those in female employment as 12.1 million, in male employment as 15.2 million, and classified female employment according to the age of dependant children and the nature of employment (full-time or part-time). The report broke down the family status of women in the UK labour market as shown in Figure 3.1.

Of note are the totals: 61 per cent of the UK women had no children under age of 18; 3 per cent had children in the age range 16–17; 9 per cent had children in the age range 11–15; 13 per cent with children in the 5–10 year age range; and 14 per cent with children in the 0–4 age range. Fifty-six per cent of the women worked full-time and 44 per cent worked part time. Women with children below the age of 11 worked part-time jobs twice as often as those who worked full-time. The statistic reversed for women with children above age 11 (including those with no children

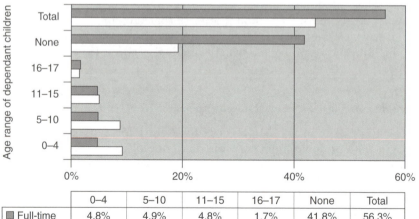

	0–4	5–10	11–15	16–17	None	Total
■ Full-time	4.8%	4.9%	4.8%	1.7%	41.8%	56.3%
□ Part-time	9.2%	8.8%	5.1%	1.5%	19.2%	43.7%

Employed women (%)

Figure 3.1 Family status of women in UK labour market.

below 18 years of age), that is, these women worked full-time jobs twice as often as they worked part-time jobs. Interestingly, the UK government did not publish the breakdown of male employment by age of dependant children. Seventy per cent of working-aged women were employed in the UK (up 1.7 per cent from 1999) and 80 per cent of working-aged men were employed (down 0.5 per cent from 1999).

Patrick McCurry (2000), commenting on the long hours and high stress levels within the workforce, states that part of the reason for today's pressures is the changing character of the workforce:

> It is estimated that the number of lone parents has more than tripled between 1971 and 2000, 43% of which are in employment. Meanwhile, six out of ten two-parent families are dual-earners, and a growing number of people who work also care for a relative.

McCurry comments that, partly in response to these changes, there have been a number of government initiatives and EU legislations, such as rights for part-timers and parental leave. He notes, however, that many employers are resisting change and quotes government statements showing that 78 per cent of employers do not allow staff to work from home, even occasionally, while only 12 per cent offer information on local child-care provision and fewer than 1 per cent offer crèches.

Care-givers in the workforce: US demographics

Roosevelt Thomas (1990) observes: 'More than half of the U.S. workforce now consists of minorities, immigrants, and women ... over the next 10 years, white males will make up only 15% of the increase in the workforce.' Far more American women are working and, typically, they are earning a lot more than they used to. While the proportion of working-age men with a job has fallen from 80 per cent in 1960 to 70 per cent in 1995, the share of women working has risen from 35 per cent to over 55 per cent. (*The Economist*, June 8, 1996). By some measures, the typical man's earnings fell by 7 per cent between 1973 and 1993; those of the typical woman rose by 11 per cent. Women are working more across the board but the biggest increase has come from women married to high-earning husbands. Perhaps the most telling finding was in the changing approach to career building. Worrell and Cooper (1999) reported that in the buoyant job market, the demands of 'Generation X' were changing. Forty per cent of high flyers said they intended to leave their employer within two years. Only 7 per cent expected to stay more than five years.

Marc Marchese, Gregory Bassham and Jack Ryan (2002) report a US Bureau of Labor Statistics (1998) finding that shows that the number of dual-worker families (families in which both husband and wife work) grew by 352,000 between 1996 and 1997 whilst the number of 'traditional' families dropped by 145,000. In 1997, the labour-force participation rate of mothers was 72 per cent, including a participation rate of 75 per cent from unmarried mothers. The US Census Bureau (2000) reports that whilst in about three out of five (60.44 per cent) married-couple families both husbands and wives work for pay, in only one out of three (34.91 per cent) do wives work full time, year round. The participation rate for mothers with a child under 1 year old grew from 54 per cent in 1996 to 58 per cent in 1997. Moreover, in 1997, 65 per cent of mothers with children under the age of 6 participated in the workforce. These figures add demographic pressure to the challenge of finding solutions for satisfactory child-care assistance for today's workers.

According to the US Bureau of Labour Statistics, the number of working mothers with children under 3 years of age rose by 9.5 per cent to 5.3 million during the 1990s. That same proportion grew by 47 per cent during the 1980s. In 2003 nearly two-thirds of mothers with children under 3 years of age are working outside their homes. That figure is up from about 50 per cent in the 1990s and 42 per cent in the 1980s. As in the UK, little seems to have been published in the USA concerning working fathers and their family status.

Many adults, mostly women, also care for ageing parents whilst continuing to provide substantial support for their children. These care-givers for the elderly are now as likely to be men as women (*Houston Chronicle*, September 25, 2000).

Karen Lee (2000) reminds us of the 'other' slice of responsibility confronted by the 'sandwich' generation: adult dependant care. She reports

---

Kyle is 38 years of age, has been employed with his firm for 16 years, has a BSc degree and works as a Senior Credit Analyst, supervising a department of fifteen staff providing support for the credit card section. He is married and his partner works full time as a Pharmacist. They have been married 5 years and have no children. Kyle is an only child and came late in his parent's life. Kyle's parents are both in poor health. His father was diagnosed with lung cancer and had surgery 2 months ago. He is still recuperating from the surgery and periodically requires treatment. Kyle's mother is in the beginning stages of Alzheimer's disease. Kyle's and his partner's lives have been disrupted by the onset of elderly care. Kyle and his partner have both taken vacation time and personal leave days to share the caring responsibilities. According to Kyle, 'the firm has been wonderful – allowing me to adjust my schedule and delegate a lot of the work to my associates so the deadlines have continued to be met. However, I don't know how long this will continue. My mother particularly will only get worse and we are looking at nursing homes for the proper care when the time comes. It is very hard to juggle high-powered careers and the care needed by your parents. We are taking it day by day.'

that benefits managers and work/life experts feel that as compared to child-care, elder-care tends to be more insidious, more complicated, longer lasting and more likely to be viewed by employees as an issue they must tackle alone. A study released by MetLife Mature Market Institute showed that nearly one-quarter of all households had at least one adult who had cared for an elderly person sometimes during the previous year. It is estimated that as the baby boomers and their parents age over the next 10 years, the number of employees caring for an adult will increase to between 11 million and 15.6 million people – about one in ten workers. The MetLife study reports that 84 per cent of the employees surveyed had to use at least some of the time during work hours to care for an adult with infirmities, even if it was just to make a phone call. In order to care for their elders, 64 per cent stated that they had used sick days or vacation time, a third reported giving up some work hours, 16 per cent were recorded as quitting their jobs completely, whilst others reported passing up promotions and extra training. Sandra Timmerman, director of the MetLife Mature Market Institute, states that unlike with child-care, 'there's something not quite as accepted about an employee going to a supervisor about adult care.' Nevertheless, Timmerman reminds: 'With the baby boomers ageing, there will be much more awareness about it [elder-care].'

Unfortunately, point-by-point comparison of data between the two countries was not possible. The governments of the two countries compile and/or publish their statistics in the breakdowns that meet the interests and needs of their own country and constituents, and the interests and needs of the various UK and US constituencies are apparently somewhat different. Suffice it to say that the evidence from both countries shows a rapid increase in the number of females entering the workforce over the past two or three decades.

Moore (1996) states that 'Insurmountable social and economic obstacles are put in the way of those who want both careers and families'. In contrast, Hakim suggests that two groups of women have emerged in the past 20 years – those that are career-oriented and those that are home-centred – and states that 'Women prefer male bosses, reject sex equality in marriage and contentedly depend on men for money as they stay secondary earners in a relationship'. Hakim's argument is of importance to our central theme of care-giving. In particular, her views raise two intertwined questions: first, why is this argument restricted to female employees and does not apply to the men who choose to stay at home? And, second, to what extent can care-giving and the conditions of employment available to care-givers be seen as a matter of free choice? These questions will be addressed in turn.

The growing male role

Adam, 42 years of age, has a BSc degree and works full time as a Senior Underwriter. His partner works part time. Adam earns 75 per cent of the household income. He has two children and is able to accept most assignments beyond normal hours that have notice and none without notice because of his family responsibilities. Adam had this to say: 'Whilst presently not hindering career development, I feel that the reasons given (my children are at ages when their schooling is most important and I have declined to move the family) will in the future curtail my career development.'

Susan Estrich (1996) made the point that women weren't the only ones who don't make it to the top. She observed that most men don't make it either. She posed the question: 'What are you willing to have less of?' Estrich replied that the answer given by men has always been their families – a lot less of their kids in exchange for more work, money, and power. She observed that we are raising a generation of females who do not see themselves as victims and a generation of men who do. She concluded that an unemployed mother is likely to see unemployment as a chance to spend time with the kids, whereas the unemployed father is seen by both society and himself as a failure.

Susan Lewis (2001) cites a growing number of studies suggesting that men are increasingly valuing their family roles and wishing to be actively involved in parenting. She comments that although women continue to retain the majority of family caring work, there are shifts in men's family involvement and their willingness to modify work for family, particularly among the younger generations. This is supported by Kelly (1991), who reports that some men, as well as women, opt for changing the definition of success so as to have a greater balance between home and work. She cites findings by the recruiting firm of Robert Hall International that claims that 56 per cent of the men surveyed 'would give up a quarter of their salary to have more family or personal time'. Kelly presents statistics that show that US men were doing 30 per cent of the housework in the 1980s compared with 20 per cent in the 1960s, and that more men are becoming the primary child provider (18 per cent) while their wives are working. The UK Industrial Tribunal ruled in November 2001 that an employer who had denied a male employee's request to work part time so that he could look after his son in the afternoons was discriminated against because the employer had offered part-time jobs to female employees who had children. The case was brought to the tribunal by the equal-opportunities commission, which felt that it was the first ruling of its kind. The effect of care-giving responsibilities upon careers is largely unaddressed in the more complete sense – that is, the careers of all care-givers, female or male. The fact that care-givers can be male as well as female had received little attention – except as the 'dead-beat dad' stereo-types regaled in the media – until David Popenoe's (1996) *Life Without Father* broadened the debate.

More men are now obtaining custody of their children in divorce cases than in the past (15 per cent in the USA and 5 per cent in the UK – with both percentages growing). The US Census Bureau's Statistical Brief (April 1994) cites the increasing numbers of children who are receiving care from their fathers – 20 per cent in 1991, up from 15 per cent in 1988. Census data reflect that father care became more common between 1991 and 1998 and that care by 'family day care' providers (that is, care in the homes of non-relatives) became less frequent, dropping from 24 per cent to 18 per cent of all primary preschooler care arrangements. The US Census Bureau (*Current Population Reports*, September 1997) reports that by fall of 1993 the number of fathers caring for their children aged 0 to 14 years during mothers' working hours had risen to 14.8 million (20 per cent) and that 13 per cent were regarded as the primary care provider. Subdivided for fathers caring for their preschool children (up to the age of 5), the percentage increased to 25 per cent, with 19 per cent being the primary care-giver (providing care for their children during more of the mother's working hours than did any other single care provider). As the children reached grade-school level, the percentage of fathers being primary care-givers dropped to lower than 10 per cent.

A married father's employment status makes a big difference in whether or not he provides care for his preschool children. In 1993, 58 per cent of fathers who were not employed provided care for their preschool children while their wives were working, versus 23 per cent of employed fathers currently providing the care. Fifty per cent of primary care-providing fathers were among the unemployed and 16 per cent were among the employed. The report notes that: 'If a father is unemployed or underemployed, he will have more "free" time available to care for his children.' In the spring of 1998, an estimated 14 million parents had custody of 22.9 million children under 21 years of age (US Census Bureau, 2000). Custodial mothers represented 85.1 per cent of all custo-dial parents, only 14.9 per cent being custodial fathers (statistically unchanged since 1994). Custodial parents working full-time, year-round jobs increased from 45.6 per cent in 1993 to 51.4 per cent by 1997. Custo-dial mothers working full time increased from 40.9 per cent to 46.9 per cent, whereas custodial fathers working full time increased from 70.2 per cent to 76.9 per cent. An additional 31.7 per cent of custodial mothers and 16.8 per cent of custodial fathers worked part time during 1997. In all, 78.6 per cent of custodial mothers were working during 1997 and 93.7 per cent of custodial fathers.

Finally, according to Mary Beth Grover (1999), there were at the time of her study approximately 2.1 million single fathers heading households in the USA. She quoted the chairman of a Boston-based consulting firm as saying that work/life issues have long been viewed as a women's issue and corporations have responded with family-friendly policies, yet when men attempt to invoke the policies they are looked upon as not being very committed or serious about their jobs. In the chairman's words: 'It's a workplace dirty little secret.' Kane (2002) reports researchers as finding that new fathers tend to find ways of spending time with their newborns by piecing together vacation days here and there, sick leave and accrued leave time – a process known as 'going undercover'. She quotes Joseph Pleck, Professor of Family Studies at the University of Illinois, as stating that the real action in these informal arrangements is in the minds of the new fathers. As reported by Kane, Pleck maintains that the thinking is that if the new father took time off and called it paternity leave, it would carry the connotation that he is doing it because he is less committed to his career.

The research reported in our study shows clearly that men, as well as women, are disadvantaged by care for dependants. This lends support to those who query the ubiquity of a gendered glass ceiling.

Responsibility for care-giving

The second of Hakim's questions was that asking to what extent care-giving and the conditions of employment available to care-givers can be seen as a matter of free choice. Related to this question is that of who is therefore responsible for supporting the care of dependants. Gardiner (1997) references a Watson and Fothergill (1993) study that concludes: 'It is clear that while most women who work part-time make a positive choice to do so, others feel constrained to accept it as the only realistic option.' Hakim maintains that many women actually want to centre their economic lives around home and work part time, arguing that it is a myth that women are sidelined by men at work or are kept at home these days by forces other than choice. Is the woman a free agent and able to make clear choices, or is she constrained by circumstance – the structure of the social parameters that surround her? And what about the man's choices? In so far as care-giving is concerned, the literature appears to be divided.

This debate has deep roots in social discourse. As defined by modern theorists such as Antony Giddens (1997), agency is the individual capacity to act otherwise. Barnes (2001) focuses on the use of agency in ordinary life. According to Barnes, people act voluntarily, or else under constraint, as making choices, as seeing reason, or else as not seeing it. He wrote that we see rules and we know that certain rules are there. If those rules are to our benefit as individuals, we abide by them. If they are not to our benefit then we break them or push for a change in them to better serve our needs as individuals. On the other hand, we may push for a change in the rules to greater benefit those who have similar needs to ours. These rules are enshrined in the policies and structures established by the organisation and the State, and thus any discussion of agency in this area needs to examine the constraints under which the individual makes his or her choices.

Despite the statistics pointing to the constraints that care-givers are under, a distinction can be made between the perceptions of choice and the reality of the choices available. Barring incest or rape, consenting adults (female and male) make a choice as to whether to engage in that sexual activity which can, and frequently does, produce children. The question of what constitutes 'choice', including the consequences flowing from the personal decisions to have children, may be more of a cultural-orientation question, for example, does personal 'choice' include personal responsibility for consequences flowing from personal decisions or is society itself deemed to have some responsibility for consequences flowing from personal decisions – in this case, responsibility for the children? The response appropriate for a specific society (culture) can, and does, affect how the State may react to the effect of care-giving upon careers and, hence, the State may have a larger or smaller role to play in the search for solutions. The UK and the USA would appear to have somewhat differing approaches to the relative responsibility of the individuals and the State.

Societal responsibility

Geert Hofstede (1980) examined the effects of national cultures on social and work behaviour and highlighted some of the evolving differences between the UK and the USA. Both countries are democracies and must ultimately reflect the will of those governed. The desires of the electorate and the legislation that attempts to address these desires can and does proceed at different paces in different cultures. Yet, the similarities are also great. Hofstede (1983) has calculated an indicative numerical level on each of his four dimensions of culture for the countries of France, Germany, Great Britain, Italy, Spain, Switzerland, Canada and the USA. Utilising Hofstede's numerical ratings, the 'mean absolute deviation' test was used to confirm the relative cultural closeness of the USA and Great Britain *vis-à-vis* the closeness of the USA and any of the other major economic powers of Europe or North America.

Hampton-Turner and Trompenaars (1993) sought to explain and predict how managers from seven different countries would react to conflict, why they excelled at certain jobs rather than others, and the managerial philosophies and concepts they favoured. They asserted that managers in different countries start with one of two 'values-in-tension' and described the circular nature of value resolution. They defined the impulse to individualism – 'If each individual pursues his own self interest, an invisible hand will automatically serve the common interests of the larger society' – and maintained that believers in individualism hold that if you concentrate on your own self-interest, you will automatically serve your customers and society better, which, in turn, will let you concentrate on self-interest.

Similarly, Hampton-Turner and Trompenaars defined the impulse to communitarianism – 'If the needs of the group are considered first, then the invisible hand will reach down and automatically take care of the desires of the individual' – and maintained that believers in communitarianism hold that if you concentrate on serving your customers and society better, you will automatically achieve your own personal goals, which, in turn, will let you concentrate on serving your customers and society better. Whilst pointing out that there is plenty of evidence that those who put individualism first also care about groups and organisations, and those who put organisations first also care about its individual members, they maintain that people from the same country will tend to resolve dilemmas in a similar way, as they feel that members of the same culture are likely to share common attitude because they share a common history.

In this particular context, the literature reveals that the two countries – the UK and the USA – appear to start with opposite 'values-in-tension'. Although Hampton-Turner and Trompenaars categorised the UK as commencing from the individualism position in the circular nature of value resolution, in the particular case of searching for solutions to the care-giving/career-progression conundrum the literature would appear to lend support to placing the UK in the more communitarian category as UK society, as revealed both by literature and political result, has assigned a more active role to the State. The impulse to individualism that both Hofstede (1983) and Hampton-Turner and Trompenaars (1993) attributed to the USA was consistent with the more limited role assigned by US society to the State in the search-to-date for care-giving/career-progression solutions.

Support for care-giving as a right

Before the 1980s, the UK followed more of a European approach to the supply of social services, including some provision of child-care services. Brannen and Moss (1993) advised that the Danish government made a conscious decision in the early 1960s to develop publicly funded child-care services in response to the growing number of women entering employment. They described the Danish plan as resulting in a majority of children under the age of 3 with employed parents being cared for in publicly funded child-care services. Hirsh and Jackson (1993) added: 'In Sweden, child care facilities are not only extensive but typically have realistic opening times (12 hours, from 6 a.m.).'

During the years generally referred to as 'Thatcherism', the UK started to employ more of an individual-responsibility approach to family social responsibilities. After the change of government to 'New Labour' in the mid 1990s, the UK signed the Social Contract of the European Union. This contract suggests adherence to a more communitarian approach than had been followed by the UK in its recent past. This may indicate that future UK direction in matters involving care-giving is likely to be more cognisant of European Union trends. Lucy Lloyd, of the Day Care Trust, summed it up: 'What we've achieved is a situation where it's now recognised by the [UK] government that child care is a public good that it's OK to spend private money on' (Mack, 2000).

The UK have the Employment Rights of 1996 and the Employment Relations Act, passed by Parliament in 1999, which deal with family-related issues such as paternity leave and career breaks, both of which give employees time off work for certain periods of time to deal with children and other family issues. In April 2003, as part of new legislation enacted to assist working families, a law became effective requiring employers to go through a formal process – potentially ending in a tribunal – when mothers and fathers of a child under the age of 6, or a disabled child up to the age of 18, ask for changed hours to help them combine work and family life. Employers will have the right to refuse the request on business grounds and will be obliged to show only that they have abided by the government set process of consideration. The government estimates that of the 3.8 million working parents with children under the age of 6, a further 509,000 each year will ask for changed hours, and it believes that 82 per cent (418,000) will have their request granted. Fewer than 8 per cent of parents' requests are expected to reach the tribunal (Ward, 2001).

Support for care-giving as a privilege

In contrast to the UK's leaning towards seeing support for care-giving as the responsibility of the State, in the USA the individual is seen to hold prime responsibility for care-giving. For example, The Public Agenda survey (Rasberry, 2000) concluded with statistics indicating that 53 per cent of those interviewed thought the US government should give bigger tax breaks to families in which one parent stays home, 30 per cent called for improvements in the cost and quality of child-care, while 62 per cent favoured making it easier and more affordable for one parent to stay home. The November 2000 presidential campaign in the USA and the US Federal Income tax revisions (May 2001) featured spirited debate between the two major political parties about ensuring that the majority of the benefits would flow to the 'middle class'. Both parties emphasised their commitment to the family and their willingness to assist the family with the cost of raising their children. This reflected the mainstream of political thought in the USA – citizens are free to make their individual choices but must assume the responsibilities flowing from those choices, for example, care-giving is the responsibility of the individual family and government's role is limited to assisting the family to discharge its responsibility for care-giving. Helen Blank, of the Children's Defense Fund, summed it up: 'We [the USA] don't have a systematic approach to child care because the basic bottom-line belief here is that it is a private responsibility' (Mack, 2000).

To date, US government assistance is reflected primarily in relief of some portion of the individual family unit's income taxes due plus specific (usually means tested) programmes designed to assist those near or below the poverty line. According to Barbara Galloway (2001), the USA also has a welfare system in place for those living below the poverty line that provides some assistance such as food stamps, child-care assistance and health-insurance coverage (Medicaid). Generally speaking, funds from the federal government for assistance to those near or below the poverty line are 'block granted' to the individual states and it is the individual states that design the specific programmes for implementation. In each of these 'block' grants, the federal government will usually establish some broad guidelines whilst leaving the individual states free to fashion specific programmes that reflect the needs and wishes of the people under their domain. Child-care is funded through the Child Care and Development Block Grant (US$2.1 billion) and the Child Care Entitlement to States (US$2.7 billion) (US Department of Health and Human Resources, 2003). The 2003 budget proposes US$1.3 billion for Administration on Aging programmes.

The USA has provided some recognition of family work–life stress with the passage in 1992 of the Family Leave Act (FLA). This Act provides 12 weeks of unpaid leave from work for a family-related health-and-emergency-type absence, to any or all employees who have been employed at least 26 weeks through the month before applying for the leave. It need not be child- or immediate-family related. The Act does provide right of return to job but the leave is unpaid except in the State of California, which, in September 2002, enacted legislation to provide 6 weeks' leave at 55 per cent of salary to new parents of children, natural or adopted. The leave will be paid for by employees via a tax estimated at US$2.30 per employee per month, whilst the employers will assume the cost for replacement employees. (There is debate over the cost, which has been based on current FLA usage. Many feel that the current usage will rise dramatically with the addition of the salary supplement.)

To summarise, the main difference between the UK and the US programmes relating to children and other family assistance is that the US programmes are all means (income) tested, whereas the UK child-allowance programmes (as outlined later) are available to everyone, and others, such as day-care centres, are available to many. The social and political values of the people of each country have influences on these governmental programmes. In terms of agency or the role of government (the State), in the UK people expect the government to take a vital role in programmes for their children. An example of this is a child-allowance stipend of a monthly amount is that given to each mother per child regardless of the economic status of the mother and regardless of the number of children in the family. The amount is set with a first child and a decreased amount is paid for each child thereafter. The citizens of the UK look upon these programmes more as a right than a privilege. The US concern is more focused on resources. The government is expected to assist those living below the poverty line in order that a minimum agreed level of quality of life be available to all. For those individuals and families with resources above the poverty line, the USA has generally followed the value-resolution approach associated with the impulse to individualism.

The choice about whether or not to have children is not made in a vacuum. Expectations of support differ between the USA and the UK. In reference to the UK, Brannen (1999) set forth the claim that 'in reducing child care to personal responsibility, there is an implicit assumption that children are a matter of choice rather than an intrinsic part of the adult life course and societal obligations'. She stated that if paid work is to become a prerequisite for lone parenthood in the UK, social policy needs to construct motherhood, lone or partnered, as workers and carers, a situation that exists in the Scandinavian societies. In contrast, Gloria Steinem, co-founder of *Ms* magazine and generally regarded as a radical feminist, emphasised the place of 'choice' in commenting upon her recent marriage:

> The symbols that we rebelled against – such as high heels, push-up bras, taking a man's name after marriage, quitting work to raise children – now are freely chosen, or the context has changed. Young women feel different about these things because they're freely choosing them; and, in fact, they're a form of rebellion in themselves. The core question is: Is this our choice?
>
> (Frey, 2000)

To put it in a nutshell, the UK employee may see benefits as a right, whereas the US employee may see benefits as a privilege.

Organisational support for care-givers

Perceptions and reality of choice are also influenced by organisational support, or otherwise, for care-givers – and the potential organisational support is influenced by the aspects of individual and State support discussed above. Barnett (1999) pointed out that although corporations were being exhorted to respond to the workers' non-workplace needs, the real message was that employed women with children, not employees in general, were under stress in trying to manage their child-rearing demands while meeting the workplace needs at the same time. In the 1990s, many US employers responded by installing specific work–family policies whose primary aim was to help women employees better manage the boundary between work and family. The employers' stated aim was to assist women employees to be more productive and the policies of choice included parental leave, flextime, on-site child-care, and child referral services.

Rodgers and Rodgers (1989) list four principal business reasons why corporate interest in work-and-family issues is rapidly growing. First, the workforce demographics are changing. With the baby boom over, higher costs are associated with high turnover, lost productivity and absenteeism because of a scarcity in labour. Second, employees' perceptions are changing. The traditional career path is on a collision course with employees wanting to be parents. 'Women and men in two-career and single-parent families are much better able to identify policies that will let them act responsibly toward their families and still satisfy their professional ambitions.' In two studies at Du Pont, the author found that men's reports of certain family-related problems nearly doubled from 1985 to 1988. Third, there is increasing evidence that inflexibility has an adverse effect on productivity. A study by Merck in 1984 showed that an employee with a supervisor who was unsupportive about family issues had higher levels of stress, greater absenteeism and lower job satisfaction. Other studies show that supportive companies attract new employees more easily, have quicker returns from maternity leave and have higher workforce morale. Fourth, concerns about America's children are growing fast. Poverty is up, single parenting is increasing, the Scholastic Aptitude Test (SAT) scores are falling and childhood illiteracy, obesity and suicide rates are all on the rise. Business communities have tried efforts to improve schools, whilst the Rodgers' study showed that parents said they did not have the workplace flexibility to attend teacher conferences and important school events (Rodgers and Rodgers, 1989).

There is an element of choice about whether or not to have children, but if we look at care-giving responsibilities for other dependants, such choice is not often available – parents and others get old or infirm and need to be cared for, regardless of the societal mores that influence the perceptions of who is responsible for such caring. Organisations, out of self-interest, are increasingly seeking to adopt dependant-care policies. In Hewitt Associates' 1999 survey of US employers, 90 per cent reported that they offer some kind of child-care assistance – 88 per cent offer dependant-care spending accounts; other popular child-care benefits include resource and referral services (42 per cent), sick or emergency child-care programmes (13 per cent) and on-site or near-site day care centres (10 per cent); 47 per cent offer elder-care programmes – dependant-care spending accounts (32 per cent), resource and referral services (40 per cent), long-term care insurance (17 per cent); 74 per cent offer flexible scheduling arrangements – including flextime, job sharing, telecommuting and compressed working weeks – and 52 per cent offer on-site conveniences such as banking services (22 per cent), automatic teller machines (34 per cent), travel services (18 per cent), and dry cleaners (15 per cent). Thirty-one per cent of employers offer adoption-assistance benefits, compared to 21 per cent in 1994, making adoption assistance one of the fastest growing work/life benefits offered by employers (Workforce, May 2000).

The adoption of dependant-care policies, however, has not met with universal acceptance. To Barnett, the reaction of the employers in installing family-friendly workplace policies, however well intended, reinforced the view that work and family were separate and in competition. Barnett claimed that, in practice, women who took advantage of these policies were seen as less committed and less desirable and their career-advancement opportunities at the workplace were curtailed. Barnett maintained that work and family were not two separate spheres and that policies fashioned on the separate-spheres philosophy would miss the mark (Barnett, 1999). Moen and Yu (2000) reminded us that families have always devised strategies to deal with the inevitable exigencies that occur in life. They believe that in this process there is invariably a period of structural lag, defined as a time when institutionalised customs and practices persist in the face of changing realities. They feel that workers are confronting precisely such a lag in the interface between their work and their family roles and cite as evidence the growing number of workers (both male and female) who are experiencing both workplace and domestic responsibilities. They conclude that work remains structured as if employees were without family responsibilities or other non-work-related personal involvements.

Similarly, Poe (2000) pointed out that a growing number of workers without children were dissatisfied. She reported that the resentment was fuelled by the perception that the majority of the workforce – those without young children – must cover for the minority – those with young children. Further, Poe credited many of the majority as believing that gains made in flexible arrangements and paid and unpaid leave never reached the majority of workers – those without young children. Elinor Burkett (2000) cited Bureau of Labor Statistics that reported that 60 per cent of the US workforce did not have a child in the household under the age of 18. She pointed out that the US Census Bureau data shows that 19 per cent of married couples had chosen not to have children, up from 11 per cent a decade earlier. Burkett joined Poe in claiming that there was resentment by the majority of the workforce because they must cover the absences of the minority (those with children). Rodgers and Rodgers (1989) found that the higher a woman's education level, the more likely she is to be employed and the less likely to have children. One study shows that two-thirds of the women under 40 who have reached the upper echelons in our largest companies and institutions are childless, while virtually all men in leadership positions are fathers. This raises the possibility of a backlash against family-friendly policies from those who have 'chosen' not to have children in order to further their career (Young, 1999). 'What do they think, I was hatched? Just because I'm single and have no children seems to mean I am always available to work overtime,' says Martha Fields (2001).

Henry is 24 years of age, has completed 2 years of college, works as a project manager in IT and has been with his firm for 4 years. Henry is a high-flyer and has been promoted once since coming on board. His area of responsibility includes many projects with specific deadlines and his group provides IT support for two other departments. Henry is single. His father recently died suddenly and his mother now lives with him. He has no dependant other than his mother. He has no experience in child-care or elderly-care as his mother enjoys good health. Henry is very serious about his career and works long hours. When asked about employees wanting and needing time off for care-giving responsibilities, Henry had this to say: 'I have to pick up work when someone is out for any reason and some days I have to chase people down – call home to find out where the work is so it can be finished to meet deadlines. It can be very frustrating at times, when you really need them at work and they are out taking care of their children. I am not against having children mind you. But perhaps they should transfer to a different department that does not have deadlines.'

Dolliver (2000) reports that childless employees are beginning to react against the privileges they see working parents receiving, such as flex scheduling, work-at-home days, family emergency time to tend sick children, attend PTA and soccer games and take school vacations. He states that to the childless employees it seems as if employees with children can come and go as they please. Dolliver cites a *USA Today* (national newspaper) poll showing that people think that non-parents receive preference over parents in pay, promotions, workload and plum assignments.

- nearly three in four Americans rate their own workplace as pro-family;
- four in ten working adults say they have heard a co-worker complain about parents getting a break at work with better schedules, responsibilities or expectations;
- three in ten believe it is unfair of employers to offer special benefits – such as scholarships, day care, adoption help – that not all workers can use;
- one in three Americans have covered for a co-worker who had to leave work to care for a child;
- one in three say it is a distraction when parents bring their children to work.

Dolliver concluded that the poll did not show that resentment had reached major proportions as yet. He states that when childless respondents were asked how they felt about parents getting a better deal at work, 84 per cent said they had never got angry. It seems that the respondents perceived that there were also advantages for the non-parent at the workplace. Dillner (2000) supported this view, concluding that there was little substance in the allegations that raging resentment exists.

In summary, this chapter has given an overview of the literature and statistics around care-giving. Whilst the main focus reflects that of the literature, namely child-care by women, it has also explored the implications for male care-givers and for those who provide care for other dependants. We have explored some of the differences in approach adopted in the USA and the UK, arguing that in essence, US citizens see care-giving support as a privilege, whereas UK citizens see it as a right. These points will be explored empirically in the next chapter.

4 Gender-free impact of care-giving

Previous chapters have emphasised that much of the literature about the glass ceiling alludes to 'invisible barriers' in corporations that keep women from the boardrooms (McQuarrie, 1994; Schadovitz, 1996; Jones and Causer, 1995). The focus in the literature has mainly been upon women and, to some extent, their role in child-care. We have suggested that a wider focus needs to be adopted – to include the role of men, and to include the care for other dependants. We have presented some literature, opinions and statistics about this, but have noted the lack of detailed comparable evidence across the studies that have been conducted. In this chapter we present and discuss a study that was designed to adopt the wider lens.

A study was undertaken to broaden understanding of issues and needs facing those employees who were trying to balance their care-giving responsibilities with their career aspirations. A decision was made to look beyond that crowd of activists and theorists who seek to capture the term 'glass ceiling' for the exclusive use of those who pursue discrimination theories and to embark upon a voyage of discovery. It is one thing to accept (and even admire) the elegance of the 'transparent barrier' portion of the glass ceiling description used by Powell and Butterfield (1994) but quite another to accept that its descriptive power should be limited only to the cause of discrimination. This study seeks neither to dispute nor refute the questions of discrimination against females and minorities. It does reject any attempts to claim the term 'glass ceiling' for the exclusive use of any particular cause. We seek to surface the possibility that other factors may also have bearing upon who is sitting in the boardroom.

The survey concentrated on lone parents who are both employed and have primary responsibilities for children and/or other individuals living within the same household. These lone parents also maintain primary financial and emotional responsibility for those dependants. Lone, employed parents were selected as the focus of this limited-purpose study because it was felt that this group could be a lightning rod for the range of issues affecting the care-givers' balancing act with their careers. Simply put, lone parents were likely to be experiencing the same feelings of being pulled in two directions as are felt by the employed with partners and children. However, by definition the lone parent has no partner with whom to share the responsibilities. By conducting the survey, an attempt was made to gain the greatest amount of understanding – at the 'hands on' level – in the smallest amount of time.

Because of the nature of the lone-parent study (written surveys), quantitative methodology was most useful for determining key areas of focus. The limited opportunities for 'open' responses included in the written lone-parent survey provided valuable directional support in determining areas of emphasis for the research presented in Part 2 of this book. The sample was small (135 responses), did not include respondents with other types of dependants, was focused on a single category of care-givers, and the empirical data reported reflects these limitations. As a small study, generalisability of findings was not the objective. In seeking to better understand lone parents' views concerning any relationship between their care-giving responsibilities and their job-commitment capabilities, respondents from two developed countries (the UK and the USA) were selected to participate in the survey because, as discussed above, employment practices with respect to management opportunities being presented to females and males within the two countries were known to be proceeding at different paces, yet are similar enough in broad outlook to provide some consistency of scope.

Two national lone-parent organisations participated in the survey – Parents Without Partners (USA), and Gingerbread (UK) – as well as a group of US lone-parent teachers. A criterion for membership in both organisations is being a single parent with primary care-giving responsibility for at least one dependant. Both organisations have large memberships (60,000 US members and 10,000 UK members). They are affiliate organisations with similar goals and similar programmes, all of which centre around children and family activities. Surveying these groups allowed the study of differences, if any, that may exist between the two countries in relation to the struggle of lone primary care-givers. The written survey was distributed and completed during the organisations' regular evening meetings. US members of Parents Without Partners formed the majority (sixty-two) of participants in the first study. However, a total of thirty-nine other south Florida single parents also participated; thirty-three from a teachers' group and six from a church group, all of whom met the main selection criteria. A total of 101 respondents in the USA participated. Total UK participation was 34 respondents, all from the Gingerbread organisation.

The survey was designed as a blind survey, that is, the participants would not identify themselves by name, address or other personal details. It sought closed-answer background information, opinions and feelings via a seven-point Likert scale and further comments with open questions at the end of each section. The survey design provided each respondent with the opportunity to provide information about her/himself that broadly fell into three categories: personal data; employment factors; and perception factors. The major focus of the survey was an attempt to determine whether care-giving responsibilities had adversely affected lone-parent ability to accept favourable employment opportunities (past and present) and the level of anxiety, if any, concerning future events that could adversely affect care-giving ability.

Summary of results

The main findings of the lone-parent survey were that a significant number of lone-parent respondents reported that the reality of their sole-responsibility circumstance had resulted in diminished career progress. The data examined to support this conclusion were the respondents' replies to specific factual questions ('Have you at any time, because of family responsibilities: Declined a promotion? Declined a move or transfer?') plus their replies to specific perception questions ('Do you think that the level of care you provide for dependants is hindering your career development?'; 'Do you think that the level of care you have provided for dependants in the past has hindered your career growth?'). Further, emotional concerns of the lone-parent respondents were solicited relating to the level of worry over future inability to work, to care for dependants and to cope with personal loss or grief. The literature surrounding the subject of the 'glass ceiling' appears virtually to ignore these areas yet the responses received indicate areas of concern for several of these groups.

Lone parents working to support themselves and their dependants experience unique obstacles in pursuing the twin goals of career and family guardian. UK and US responses to the career/guardian choice represented by declining offered promotions segmented by country and gender are depicted in Figure 4.1.

A higher percentage of UK respondents – both female and male – reported declining promotions than did their US counterparts. UK male respondents represented the highest percentage declining promotions, followed by UK females and US females. US males were the least affected.

The situation changes in the UK with the respondents' perceptions of hindrance of career progress – past and present. UK and US responses to the career/guardian choice by perception of experiencing present and past career hindrance, segmented by country and gender, are depicted in Figures 4.2 and 4.3.

The highest percentage of career hindrance by dependant responsibilities now and in the past was the UK female, with the UK male following close behind her. US female respondents felt career hindrance both presently and in the past to a greater degree than did their US male counterparts.

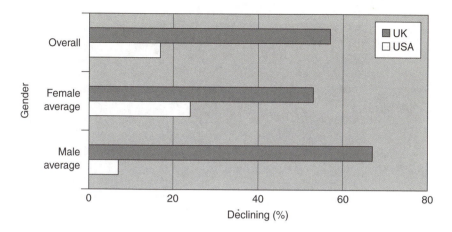

Figure 4.1 Lone-parents declining promotion – UK vs. USA.

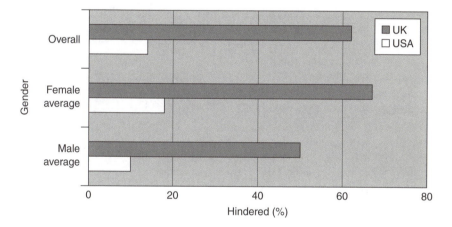

Figure 4.2 Lone-parent progress hindered by present dependant responsibilities –
  UK vs. USA.

Probing of lone parents' emotional concerns about their care-giving responsibilities was sought by requesting their indications of the extent to which they agreed or disagreed with the following statements: 'I am worried about not being able to work'; 'I am worried about not being able to care for my dependants'; 'I am worried about not being able to cope with personal loss or grief'. A seven-point Likert scale ranging from 'Strong' to 'Neutral' agreement/disagreement was provided. Segmented by country and gender, the responses for lone parents' concerns about their future ability to care for dependants are presented in Figure 4.4.

In all three areas, the UK lone-parent respondents expressed a greater

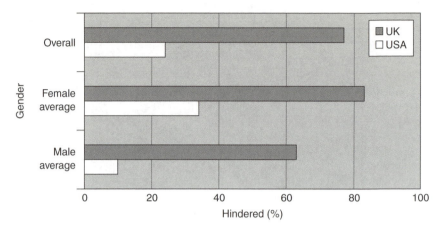

Figure 4.3 Lone-parent progress hindered by past dependant responsibilities – UK vs. USA.

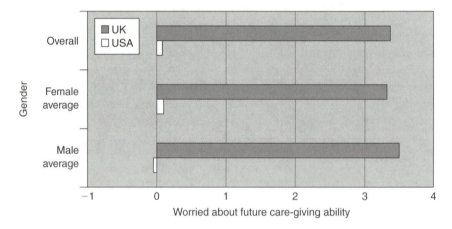

Figure 4.4 Lone-parent worries over future care-giving ability – UK vs. USA.

degree of worry about their future care-giving ability than the US respondents. UK males expressed the greatest degree of worry. US males showed negative worries in all areas, with US females showing negative worries in the coping-ability area and slight worry in the other two areas.

General comments of UK and US respondents

UK respondents mentioned the stress of sole responsibility and making decisions alone. They expressed worry about money to pay the bills. Some were concerned about becoming ill, leaving no one to care for their children. Others showed quiet determination by stating that lone parents have to cope, but noting how hard it was to do so. Most respondents reflected a desire to do more for themselves but a frustration with 'the system', which, in their opinion, shows inadequate understanding of the child-care/work dilemma faced by lone parents. They maintained that at lower levels of the organisation it is difficult to fit within the workday those child visits to the doctor, dentist, school and so on. Some would like practical support. Others were frustrated that their skills, in their opinion, were not recognised. Some feel guilty if they work and feel guilty if they don't work. One wrote that the 'benefit system provides basic care but the inability to do paid work limits my standard of living, my self esteem, and ability to be a positive role model'. Another wrote that 'not enough help is provided for lone parents with additional care-giver responsibilities with no chance to go back to work'. Some cited the inability to get child-care providers to look after children for the extended hours required to succeed (to advancement). Others feel that lone parents need support with child-care in order to get retraining, plus they say there is no back-up in cases of crisis. One wrote that single parents find it hard to get child-care and must pay for it from their meagre wages.

From these comments, it appears that UK participants are more frustrated with their system than are US participants. On the other hand, these comments could simply mean that the British parents were more open and vocal about their true feelings and more willing to express them than were the American lone parents, amongst whom an admission of requiring external financial support appears to have been more socially stigmatised. This conclusion is supported both by the differences in cultural profile discussed in the previous chapters and by the quantity and quality of open-ended responses, in which the UK participants were much more forthcoming. This difference was also seen in the closed responses about finances, in which several US respondents expressed disquiet at being asked for financial information and were unwilling to offer more than the minimum responses in this area.

The limited number of US participants' volunteering comments focused mainly on the emotional issues. One respondent wrote that if she became disabled, her family would be severely stressed – financially and emotionally. Another female respondent wrote that 'fathers get off scot-free'. According to one participant, 'it took years to become emotionally free'. Some reported that they worked it out. Others said they are not worried. A few were quite candid about the survey itself, including comments such as 'I found it unpleasant to fill out'. Some felt that 'other benefits' were none of the researcher's business. Another participant suggested forgetting the check boxes on the survey form and said 'just ask me, I've been through it all'. Yet verbally, many of the respondents confided that the number-one difficulty to be overcome as a lone parent was finding, becoming comfortable with and funding appropriate arrangements for child-care during work time.

Findings and interpretations

The overarching finding of this lone-parent survey is its confirmation of the common suspicion that a major obstacle to lone-parent attainment and/or acceptance of corporate promotions and qualification-building transfers is the existence of family-related 'external' (non-work-connected) factors that have unique power to impact lone parents' working lives – gender notwithstanding. Other primary care-givers are also affected, namely, dual breadwinner families and/or families where one partner assumes the primary care responsibility. Principle findings from the lone-parent survey were: (1) in the situation of lone parenthood, males reported encountering similar factors (problems) and/or stresses as did females; (2) both genders reported career progress being hindered by dependant responsibilities – both presently, and even more so in the past; (3) UK respondents reported significantly greater hindrance (past and present) than US respondents (both genders). The results from the survey were augmented by a generous number of volunteered written comments, especially from the UK.

Throughout the survey runs the refrain that care-giving responsibilities are rated by the respondents as being of the highest order – above that level of responsibility owed to an employer for accepting potentially life-style-altering promotions or transfers and/or of pursuing the perform-ance levels that merit consideration for career advancement.

> **Gertrude** is 32 years of age, has a BSc degree and works full time in a cleri-cal position that requires her to work 43 hours per week and travel an addi-tional 5 hours per week to and from work. She is divorced and has one child in preschool. She has not had any career-development training but has not sought any. She does not see that care-giving has had a negative impact. Gertrude is usually able to accept assignments outside of normal hours that have prior notice given, but pop-up assignments without notice are more difficult because she has to pick up her child. When asked if her employer understands and supports her care-giving situations, she moderately dis-agreed and said she was only slightly comfortable invoking the policies in place for care-givers. When asked if her care-giving arrangements were com-patible with her employers' expectations for promotions, she replied: 'To move up would require sacrificing more time from my family.' When asked if she was maximising her professional potential, she replied 'No. However, my priorities have changed – now I have a family.'

The data indicate that lone parents in the UK appear to be more nega-tively impacted in their careers by their care-giving responsibility than US lone parents. They also appear to be more concerned about their eco-nomic and emotional future. However, as discussed above, this might be a relative effect of the different cultures, in which less stigma is attached to admitting the need for economic support in the UK than in the USA. Similarly, findings of more hours worked, more travel, possibly even more frequent receipt of a company car by the US respondents may say more about the present state of the respective economic culture of the two countries than about lone parents with unique problems. However, different government policies in areas of eligibility for government benefits, limitations on work, government payment eligibility criteria and so on could also contribute to the difference in work hours.

The more generous assistance given to single parents (both female and male) in the UK seems to have spawned a mixed blessing for its recipients. Greater UK governmental support may possibly explain the ability of UK respondents to decline promotions or transfers to a greater degree than US respondents. However, finding that the UK respondents were also more worried about their future ability to work, to care for dependants and to cope with loss was surprising in view of the presumed greater social safety net enjoyed by them. This finding could also be influenced by the fact that the UK respondents were more open in their comments and replies than the US respondents. As their comments suggested, the US respondents were less expressive of their feelings on this subject and some saw the survey itself as an invasion of their privacy.

The level of perceived hindrance to career caused by care-giving responsibilities in the present was noticeably lower than the level of perceived hindrance in the past for both UK and US groups. The majority of UK managerial/professional male respondents felt hindered in both the past and the present, while few similarly situated US males professed these feelings. The managerial/professional males also differed strongly on declining promotions, worry over future inability to care for dependants and to cope with personal loss. In each of these areas UK managerial/professional males felt greater impact than their US counterparts. These two comparisons give some support to a very tentative finding that females at the managerial/professional level, in both the UK and the USA, may be making some progress (however glacial) in their battle to handle the demands of both career development and family guardianship. The findings reveal a US managerial/professional male that says he is relatively confident of juggling both career and guardianship responsibilities, whilst a UK managerial/professional lone-parent male says he is considerably less so.

Overall comparison of the responses from the two countries might indicate that the recognition by organisations of care-giving responsibilities and the impact on employment prospects of single parents is more advanced in the USA than in the UK. It appears that US employers may be more aware of the need to extend tangible assistance to this growing group of talented employees in order to obtain and retain them.

Of perhaps greater interest, however, is not the differences that exist between the two countries but the similarities that are present. It is noteworthy throughout that the problems of lone parenthood impact in a similar manner amongst the males and females of this study, regardless of their nationality. In other words, these problems and their effects upon perceptions of career progression are gender neutral.

Conclusion

The findings of this survey add strength to the proposition that lone parents encounter stresses and problems that can and do adversely impact on their careers regardless of their gender. If these conflicting forces represent a nucleus of career-limitation reasons for males not achieving higher career levels, do males also experience the 'glass ceiling'? If males can experience a glass ceiling, does the definition of 'glass ceiling' need to be revised to include males? If the glass ceiling includes males, then much of the gender-related sting is removed from this late-twentieth-century buzz-word for gender discrimination. Possibly the 'ceiling' is more of a 'net' that catches those, regardless of gender, who no longer strive (for whatever reason) to make an all-consuming effort to swim upstream and be amongst the few to reach the great salmon-spawning grounds. Career-wise, the great spawning grounds might be better known as the 'top management club'.

   Care-giving responsibilities are not the sole preserve of the lone parent. Talented, married, single- and/or double-breadwinner families can also place the demands of care-giving or other non-company-connected responsibilities above the perceived demand to put the company first. In the following part further empirical evidence is presented that builds upon the findings discussed here, and which broadens the debate to explore the possible effects of care-giving across the wider population.

Part II

Some empirical evidence

The previous part laid the groundwork for an investigation of the effect of care-giving upon career and showed that the impact of care-giving was gender-free – at least in the case of lone parents. That research was undertaken primarily to obtain greater understanding of the issues involved in care-giving; therefore it was non-random, and relatively small. The issues it raised, however, are much larger, and the lack of comparable empirical evidence in this area has laid the ground for wider and more structured research.

To date, primary evidence on the subject of care-giving and career advancement seems to be in rather scant supply. Works citing secondary evidence and/or bold opinions are plentiful indeed. Yet, according to Weiers (2002), 'Secondary data have been gathered by someone else for some other purpose'. The validity of secondary data is not in question, though the need to interpret and apply it can have its pitfalls. The primary data presented in this part was obtained specifically for the purpose of addressing the questions posed here and thus such interpretative pitfalls are minimised. Chapter 5 briefly details the research population and methodology adopted. The following chapters explore different foci arising from the research, namely, the impact that care-giving has upon perceived commitment to work (Chapter 6), upon development opportunities (Chapter 7), upon career attainment (Chapter 8) and upon the balance between time available and freedom to pursue a career (time/freedom) (Chapter 9).

Because of the nature of book writing (and reading), we felt that an overabundance of statistical data might not enhance the experience for the reader. Therefore, the presentation of the empirical research discussed here is done (it is hoped) in an accessible and reader-friendly manner. Readers who are keen to obtain further details are referred to Coyne (2001) or are invited to contact the authors of this book.

5 The need for empirical data

This chapter steps to one side of the main lines of argument in the book in order to provide details of the research design, methodology and population upon which the main lines of argument are based. These are necessarily presented in a brief form, and further details can be found in Coyne (2001).

The research population

As discussed in Chapter 3, the UK and the USA have broadly similar cultures but different laws, customs, and practices affecting the workplace. Industrial and service-sector development within the two countries has developed at different paces. National employment needs and available qualified people to fulfil those needs are different for the two countries. Therefore, it was felt that a comparison of these two countries would facilitate an examination of the effect of work practices without the added confusion arising from widely differing cultures.

An investigation into whether care-giving is 'an upper limit to professional advancement that is not readily perceived or openly acknowledged' necessitates that the industry subjected to the investigation employ both women and men as both are involved in the care-giving process. The search was for an industry that was 'average-modern' in the developed-country sense (one that utilised modern technology in everyday operation – yet was neither 'high tech' nor 'low tech' in nature). The banking sector was chosen for the investigation because the services industries have emerged as the largest segment of economic activity, utilising 74 per cent of the labour force in both the UK and the USA. (*The Economist, Pocket World in Figures,* 2003). Furthermore, within the services sector the banking industry historically has maintained a reputation for being a gender neutral employer. The following brief review tends to confirm both of these assumptions.

In June 2000, 74 per cent of the UK's 28 million person workforce was engaged in the service industries. The Office of National Statistics defines service industries as being composed of public administration, education and health (30.9 per cent); distribution, retail and restaurants (29 per cent); finance and business services (24.5 per cent); transportation and communications (8 per cent); and other (7.7 per cent). Eighty-seven per cent of all female workers are employed in the service industries and 65 per cent of all male workers (derived from Employment, Earnings and Productivity Division report, ONS, B18). In total, females make up 44 per cent of the services workforce and men 56 per cent. Within the UK finance and business sector, the female/male breakdown is 48.4 per cent/51.6 per cent. The US Equal Employment Opportunity Commission (EEO) (1999) reports the total employment in depository institutions (Standard Industrial Code #60) as 1,104,844, segmented as 68 per cent women and 32 per cent men.

This book offers some quantitative and qualitative empirical data, gained from 553 surveys and thirty interviews with male and female executives representing all career levels within six major banks in the UK/US banking industry. The desire was for banks that collectively would be representative of the banking industry in both countries. The type of banking activity conducted by the bank – for example, commercial, merchant, savings and loan (or the UK equivalent of building societies) – was *not* a factor considered in recruiting banks for the project. The prime concern was to recruit banks that would be representative of the employment and career-development practices being utilised within the industry; thus banks that were large employers with multiple branches were accessed.

All three UK banks participating in this research are included the nine-bank Major British Banking Groups sector as defined by the British Bankers Association (BBA). The BBA web page states: 'These banks [Major British Banking Groups] account for around three-quarters of sterling domestic business undertaken by the banking sector and therefore information on the balance sheet and lending can be considered representative of all retail banking activity' (BBA, 2001). All three US banks participating in this survey are located in the southeast region of the USA. According to the US Census (2000), the combined population of this eleven-state region is approximately 68 million people (24 per cent of the US population). Each of the banks is included in the 'Top 25 US Banks' category (that is, the largest twenty-five banks), as determined by market capitalisation. As full service banks, they compete with most of the banks included in the Top 25 category. At least four of the Top 10 have home offices within the southeast region and many of the Top 25 have branch operations within the region (Wright Investor's Services, 2001).

There is strong reason to believe that the sample population of the participating UK and US banks fairly represents both the banks themselves and the national banking sector of each country, in so far as they reflect a fair and representative ratio of female and male employees. Labour Market Trends (UK) (June 2001) lists employment in the financial and business services industry and these figures have been used as a rough estimate for the banking industry, recognising that the business services portion of this industry grouping may not be as weighted toward female employment as the banking sector itself. In the case of the US banking industry sector, the Federal Deposit Insurance Corporation (FDIC), which monitors all federally insured commercial banks, provides data both by gender employed and by job-level distribution, grouped into four classifications, within the banking industry. Figure 5.1 depicts the results of a comparison by country and gender of the populations in the research sample, the participating banks and national banking averages.

There is also support for a reasonably representative sample population with relation to job-level distribution as compared to the national banking sector job-level distribution of the USA. The predominance of the service sector in the economic life of both countries is evident and the banking/financial portion of the service sector is strongly represented in both countries. There is some confidence that the findings reported here might also have some generalisability to the wider employed population – especially within the services sector.

Overview of methodology

The effects of care-giving upon career development in the UK and US banking industry covers a number of areas and remains broad, controversial and susceptible to the emotional interpretations of the participants (including the authors). For these reasons it was felt that a triangulation approach – including demographics, quantitative, and qualitative data analysis – would provide a higher degree of validity to the research. Quantitative methods of analysis were used as an aid to establish the normative

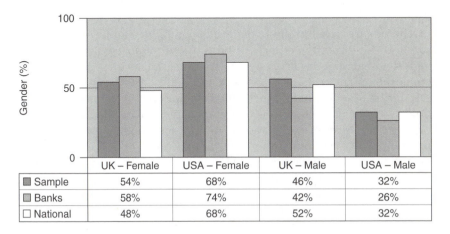

	UK – Female	USA – Female	UK – Male	USA – Male
■ Sample	54%	68%	46%	32%
▨ Banks	58%	74%	42%	26%
□ National	48%	68%	52%	32%

Figure 5.1 Comparison of female/male sample population with participating banks and sector average.

aspects of the sample and to discover areas of statistically significant differences and similarities within the sample population. Analyses of secondary sources of data were conducted to relate these findings to the wider population, and thus to the normative baseline. Qualitative methods of analysis were employed in the search for explanations of the uncovered phenomena.

Quantitative analysis is concerned with the search for norms and statistically significant variations from the norm. Qualitative analysis seeks the exceptions to the norms and focuses on 'why'. The dual approach adopted in this research sought 'the best of both worlds' while recognising the existence of vigorous debate on the appropriate methodologies to be employed in the social sciences and the differing 'world views' that underpin these methodological stances.

Broadly, the debate centres on three different philosophical stances. A positivistic approach holds that social science differs little from the natural sciences and that 'the world is objectively and unproblematically available and capable of being known by the systematic application of the empirical techniques common to positivism' (Ackroyd and Fleetwood, 2000). A postmodern (and/or a poststructuralist) approach holds that the world is not objectively knowable and supports 'the idea that what is known is merely the product of discourse'. The third philosophical approach, that of realism, attempts to cut across the boundaries set by the more extreme possibilities of positivism and postmodernism and evidences a lengthy heritage of application in the field of management and organisation studies. '[Realism] is characterised by the conviction that social structures (mechanisms, relations, power, rules, resources, institutions, and so on) as well as the meanings that actors and groups attribute to their situation (along with the discourse used to convey these meanings), must be taken into account in any explanation of events' (Ackroyd and Fleetwood, 2000).

The subject matter of this book involves both the natural world and the social world – from the miracle of birth, the unstoppable ageing process and the material resources required for sustenance of remunerated employment and the socially mandated rights, privileges, duties and responsibilities surrounding such employment. The subject matter is emotionally charged. Charges and counter-charges of discrimination, level playing fields, sexism, exploitation and more seem automatically to attach themselves to any enquiry into even the narrowest of areas of investigation. Further, the surveys and interviews conducted in pursuit of this research into care-giving and its effect on career development has netted a broad range of data that offer many avenues for exploration. As a cross-cultural study, many areas for comparison presented themselves – country, gender, care-giving status were compared on a broad range of issues from age, education and marital (or partnered) status to job-level accomplishment, management training, mentoring, promotion and so on.

In order to maintain focus, a quantitative method was used for analysis of the 'hard' data provided by the written surveys. This quantitative technique was selected both to facilitate the pinpointing of areas where objective evidence indicated that significant differences existed between the compared groups and to examine more closely selected areas for evidence of causal relationships. However, written surveys provide only the crudest of opportunities for speculating on the veracity of the evidence being offered. They provide a broad picture of the area but little insight into the feelings, choices and individual reflections that might throw light upon what is really happening.

Qualitative techniques were brought to bear in areas that were suspected of holding clues for ferreting out potential explanations, especially in those key career-building areas where causal relationships seemed most unlikely. Face-to-face in-depth interviews, at minimum, offer the interviewer the opportunity for separating truth from 'political correctness' or other 'reasons' that might interfere with the interviewee's motivation for telling it like it is. The emphasis during the qualitative analysis phase was on 'why'. To this degree, the methodological approach adopted for this research has some common ground with the critical realist approach (with the emphasis on explanations) but with a rather deep bow to the positivists and their statistical rigour. We take no position on any of the issues *per se*. We do pose a series of questions and policy issues that can lead to further research and vigorous debate. We view our task as one of bringing empirically gathered evidence and facts surrounding the effects of care-giving upon career advancement to the ever-widening group of participants in the national debate – to the activists, to the policy makers (corporate and legislative), to the human resource practitioners, to our fellow academics and, yes, to all those being impacted – one way or another – now or in the future – by the human necessity of the care-giving experience.

The banks were asked to participate in three ways: first, to allow employees chosen at random to complete a written survey; second, to allow a small number of their executives to participate in a short executive interview; and third, to allow an HR specialist to participate in an interview about the bank's HR policies as well as to provide copies of those policies for the benchmarking aspect of the research project. Also each bank was asked for demographic information in order to determine comparability within the banking industry of the two countries and the representativeness of the sample population. The survey was designed with questions for quantitative and qualitative analyses. The interview data were appropriate for qualitative analyses.

Corporate care-giver responsibility engagement

The participating banks had little or no involvement with their employees in the provision of or remuneration for care facilities. All respondents indicated that care-giving facilities were self-provided by the employee. One UK and one US bank offered a care-provider referral service for the convenience of their child-care-giver employees but none offered referral services in the elder-care area. One UK bank offered on-site child-care at some of its facilities (the remainder of the banks reported having none). All banks offered part-time schedules and flextime. Most offered some telecommuting/working from home under various circumstances. All offered some version of paid time off for family-related issues (one US bank counted it as personal leave). Paid maternity/paternity leave was offered by the UK banks and some US banks, whilst other US banks utilised sick time or personal leave for providing pay. All offered unpaid maternity/paternity leave. Two UK and one US bank had issued a formal company statement to their employees on the importance of work/family issues.

Survey respondents – demographics

The five banks participating in the written-survey portion of the study made a conscious effort to have the sample reflect the demographics of their employees. Respondents were chosen randomly from their employee data bank. Assuming the sample represents the banks' population, females represent the majority of respondents in the UK/US banking industry and males represent a greater proportion of the UK banking industry than they do in the US Labor Market Trends, 2001, and US Federal Deposit Insurance Corporation (FDIC) data confirm both interpretations.

The age of respondents in the UK and US banking industry were similar. Male respondents were generally older than female respondents in both countries. Respondents with care-giving responsibilities were generally older than those respondents without these responsibilities. However, the age of the non-care-giver/care-giver may be more impacted by the respondent's marital status than by his or her care-giving status. The incidence of care-giving responsibilities appears to have been similar for both UK and US respondents. Part-time workers within the UK were more likely to have care-giving responsibilities (88 per cent) than were their full-time counterparts (50 per cent) in the UK. No difference between full-time and part-time US respondents of care-giver status was recorded. UK banking relied more heavily on part-time workers than did the US banking industry. The part-time labour force of the participating banks in both countries was made up predominantly of females. The majority of part-time respondents had care-giving responsibilities, more so in the UK than in the USA.

Females in the USA had caught up with US males in educational attainment but not, to date, in the UK. Whilst no statistically significant difference in educational level existed between male care-givers and non-care-givers of the two countries, female non-care-givers in both the UK and the USA were more highly educated than their care-giving counterparts. Females were also more likely to have working spouses (partners) than males. In the banking industry sample full-time working spouses were more prevalent in the USA than in the UK. Care-givers had working spouses more frequently than non-care-givers. No statistically significant differences were found for care-givers with a working spouse between UK or USA or between male or female. Within non-care-givers, females more frequently had working spouses than males.

Non-care-givers earned a greater percentage of family income than did care-givers, but both UK non-care-givers and care-givers earned a greater percentage of family income than did their US counterparts. No differences existed between the UK and the USA within the female groups of care-givers and non-care-givers, but the combined UK/US female non-care-givers were responsible for more of the family income than the combined female care-givers. The same pattern existed among the UK/US male groups. The male group was responsible for a higher percentage of the family income than the female group within the UK. In the USA the burden was more evenly shared between the genders. Korenman and Neumark (1991), Loh (1996) and Gray (1997) have all found that married men earned higher wages than unmarried men. Blau and Beller (1988) and Waldfogel (1997) found that married women also enjoyed an earnings advantage.

The data showed no statistical difference in the household presence of children for whom care-giving responsibilities exist. The respondents to this survey indicated elder-care responsibilities in only 6 per cent of the cases (the same percentage for both the UK and the USA). In trying to reconcile these interpretations of elder-care prominence with that of the literature, the key may be in the definition. This survey solicited feedback on care-giving responsibilities for children living with the same household and other family members dependent upon the employee. In spite of a number of articles suggesting that elder-care is rapidly approaching the crisis point for the 'sandwich' generation (families having both child-care and elder-care responsibilities), little evidence of this was found to exist in the UK/US banking-industry sample. Whilst some articles (Hordern, 1996; Rodgers and Rodgers, 1989) have suggested that some 33 per cent of all working families are (or soon will be) involved with elder-care, the respondents to this survey indicated elder-care responsibilities in only 6 per cent of the cases. The explanation may lie in a misinterpretation of the question 'Do you have other family members or relatives who are primarily dependent on you?' Respondents may have assumed that these dependants also must live within the same household. However, volunteered comments from the respondents about child-care were many whilst comments about elder-care were minimal.

At the moment, the banks that participated in this research project seem to be making a concerted effort to assist in addressing a number of the child-care concerns of their employees. Elder-care received some mention but did not appear to have reached far up the ladder of corporate concerns. The low percentage of respondents involved with elder-care could help explain why elder-care has not yet reached the corporate 'radar' screen of the banks participating in the research.

Years of service with employer

UK banking respondents had more service time with their present employer than did the US banking respondents. However, US respondents had more prior employer experience. Males in the UK had longer tenure than females but no significant difference existed between the genders in the USA. In both the UK and the USA, care-givers had longer tenure than non-care-givers except in the female gender, where no difference between care-givers and non-care-givers was apparent. This exception may reflect the reality that females alone possess the birthing ability and a career 'time out' of some (varying) duration is required or desired. The opportunity to speculate as to why care-giver tenure generally exceeds non-care-giver tenure has been resisted as it is beyond the scope of this work. However, it is a fit subject for further research. In all, usable returns from the written primary survey were a very robust 44.2 per cent (553 usable returns). The UK response was 53 per cent, ranging from 68.4 per cent to 40.4 per cent. The US response rate was 33 per cent, ranging from 40.4 per cent to 24.8 per cent. No unusable returns were received.

Executive interviews

The banks encouraged their executives to participate in the executive interviews as well as encouraging their employees to participate in the written survey. It was specified that executive interviews should include females and males who held either a senior management position or a supervisory position that had an impact on the bottom line of the bank. No other requirement was stated. Executives chosen to participate in the interviews were officers of the bank and/or held a banking position considered managerial in nature. The executive-interview respondents were selected for interview because their positions were of the appropriate level, they were available to speak with the researcher on the day and within the time-frame needed to complete the research and their offices were located within the city housing the operating headquarters of the bank. All thirty executives appeared as scheduled for the executive interviews, as did the six HR specialists. All interviews proceeded as scheduled and no interviews were cut short. Several interviews did exceed the scheduled 30 minutes. However, where this occurred, the scheduled time was exceeded with the acquiescence of the interviewee and usually at the instigation of the interviewee.

In summary, the empirical evidence was obtained through both qualitative and quantitative methods and was derived from a randomly distributed written survey, company documentation and interviews. The research population was derived from three US and three UK banks, and was representative of the total employees of those banks, as well as of the total banking sector in the two countries. The findings from this work are discussed in the following chapters in this part of the book.

6 Care-giving and perceptions of commitment

This chapter presents some of the findings from the research outlined in the previous chapter. It examines the perceptions that care-givers and others have about the perceived commitment to the organisation, and concludes that the ability to generate the perception of commitment (as demonstrated by long hours and instant availability) is an important element in career progression that is not as available to care-givers.

Jeffery, 32 years old, is married, has one child, a BSc degree, and works full time: He is a Senior Financial Analyst whose partner also works full time. He said 'I have to pick up our daughter at nursery. If I'm late, there's an extra charge. I can't work the extra hours so I'm not seen as committed. No commitment, no promotion.'

The perception that long hours equate with 'commitment' is endemic. Cary Scott (1997) quoted Tessa Jowell, UK minister for public health, as lamenting,

> This awful long-hours culture we have, where your effectiveness is measured not by how much you achieve but by how much time you put in, is terribly destructive of family life. It's one of the reasons that women step sideways when they see the price of success is 18 hours in the office, never being at home.

Elizabeth McKenna (1997), a former high achiever in the US publishing industry, put it this way: 'We have to ask ourselves what is more important – looking good in the eyes of our company (long hours) or working in ways that cut down the stress of having home and personal lives.' Large and Saunders (1995) reported as typical the following interview quote: 'Within the company, only full-timers are seen as committed and, if you are not seen to work later than 5:30, you are not loyal and committed.' Rodgers and Rodgers (1989) stated that another essential step required for better recognising the work of working parents was to reduce the tendency to judge productivity by time spent at work. For many hardworking people, hours certainly do translate into increased productivity. But not for all. They maintained that dismissing those who spend fewer hours at the workplace as lacking dedication ignores the fact that virtually all employees go through periods when their working hours and efficiency rise or fall, whether the cause is family, health or fluctuating motivation. Moen and Yu (2000) summed it up: 'The only way you show [job] commitment now is through long hours. The fact that seniority no longer means security means somebody has to look committed even if they're not committed.'

> Employers still feel that working conditions require adherence to a rigid 40-hour workweek, a concept of career path inconsistent with the life cycle of a person with serious family responsibilities, notions of equality formed in a different era, and performance-evaluation systems that confuse effort with results by equating hours of work with productivity.
>
> (Rodgers and Rodgers, 1989)

Moen and Yu (2000) pointed out that the 40-hour week dates back to the (US) Fair Labor Standards Act of 1938, when it defined the standard 40-hour workweek and mandated overtime pay while exempting professional occupations. Moen and Yu concluded that the act had changed little since 1938 and that 'we take this template . . . and act as if it's God-given'.

These views are supported by HR managers in this study. For example, a response from one of the UK HR specialists was:

> Our culture reinforces long hours (imitate their bosses') plus employees' own personal motivation (job security and future progress). Due to cost saving measures, people are having to work longer and harder. Where it's difficult to plan ahead, flexibility is required and employees 'able and willing' to work extra hours are a form of flexibility. EU Working Time Directive attempts to cap this. Bank policies requiring internal posting (advertising) of job vacancies attempts to take out supervisor bias toward specific employees but performance and achievement reports reflect supervision's evaluation. Most managers are now waking up to the fact that flexibility is needed, particularly for employees with family commitments.

Similarly, one of the US HR specialist responded:

> 'If the bank knows that the person plans to stay and make a career in banking, they will give career development and training to anyone. Sometimes long hours are involved for career development itself (classes are generally held outside of working hours). Career development generally is personal for that employee and the employee

should ask and seek training and career development. Career development is viewed as a 'push' and not a 'pull' system. Long hours are not formally required but supervisory judgement in completing the performance evaluations usually reflect a supervisor's view of the commitment to the job displayed by the evaluated person. That view is generally coloured by the hours the employee spends at work. We try to keep the focus on results accomplished by the evaluated person but, in truth, hours spent on the job overlay the results evaluation.

The survey responses also showed a strong perception that career development and promotion are closely linked to 'commitment' and that commitment is seen as meaning the 'ability and willingness to work extra-hours'.

Figure 6.1 reveals that average hours worked per week by the respondents in the banking industry were longer in the USA than in the UK. This finding is supported by Reich (2000), a former US Secretary of Labor, who reports the International Labour Organisation as saying in 1999 that the typical American is working 350 more hours a year than the typical European. Current EU directives concerning permissible work hours would seem to suggest that this difference is likely to continue. Males worked longer hours in the UK but no statistically significant differences in hours worked between the females and males were reported in the USA.

Figure 6.2 shows that non-care-givers reported more hours worked than care-givers with the US respondents reporting more hours worked than UK respondents in both groups. Female non-care-givers worked more hours per week than care-givers in UK/USA. US females worked more hours than UK females. There is no statistical significant difference between the males either between the UK/USA or between non-care-giver and care-giver categories. UK male care-giver respondents worked significantly more hours than their female counter parts. Over 65 per cent of UK

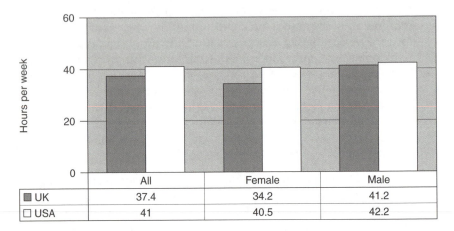

	All	Female	Male
■ UK	37.4	34.2	41.2
□ USA	41	40.5	42.2

Figure 6.1 Average hours worked per week.

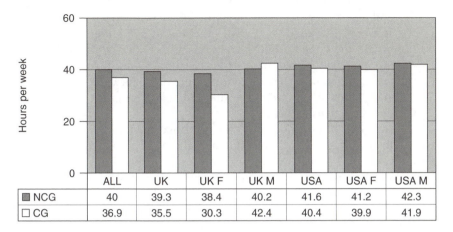

Figure 6.2 Average work hours per week – non care-givers vs. care-givers.

care-giver males have non-gainfully employed partners or partners working part-time whilst over 80 per cent of UK care-giver female respondents reported partners working full-time. UK non-care-giver respondents showed a slight difference between the females/males but did not meet the required degree of confidence level. No statistically significant differences between the hours worked by females/males in the USA were developed in either of the categories.

Ability to work extra hours – with and without notice

Josephine has a Masters degree in Business Administration, is also a Certified Public Accountant and holds a senior executive position with her firm. She is 41 years old, divorced and has custody of her two children. She supervises and has responsibility for a large section of the firm. She has been with the firm 12 years and has worked in the accounting industry for a number of years also. Josephine discussed her child-care responsibilities with me – 'When the children were younger, it was very difficult. I had a nanny, which I was thankful for, but if the children developed a fever or got hurt at day care, I would have to pick them up. I was constantly taking work home and working all hours of the night to stay ahead. Now that they are older, I have a full-time housekeeper, who is wonderful. She cleans the house, makes the meals and transports the children to their various activities for me. I am just thankful that I can afford her, because my parents live 6 hours away by car. The children spend a couple of weeks with them each summer, but other than that, I am on my own. I feel for those young families who cannot afford the luxury of help. My heart goes out to them. Because it is a constant worry – your children – are they okay? Are they being well taken care of? It causes a tremendous amount of guilty feelings when you leave them.'

There are significant differences between and among the various groups in the ability to work overtime or extra hours with notice and without notice; however, the ability to accept overtime or extra-hour assignments was essentially the same for both conditions, with notice or without notice. US respondents had greater ability to accept extra work than UK respondents, males more than females, non-care-givers more than care-givers and female non-care-givers more than female care-givers. Figure 6.3 depicts the reported situation.

The only exception to the non-care-giver acceptance superiority trend is that male care-givers reported greater ability to accept overtime with notice than male non-care-givers. However, the established pattern of non-care-givers' greater ability returns in the case of accepting overtime without prior notice of the requirement, as the male non-care-givers reported superior ability to accept than the male care-givers. As would be expected, the ability to accept overtime assignments declined for all groups when prior notice was not given and declined at a faster rate for particular groups (UK; females and all care-givers). When considered along with the prior findings of (a) longer hours worked by the UK male compared to the UK female and (b) the greater presence of a non-gainfully employed partner in the UK male respondent household, this superior ability of the UK male, as compared to the UK female, to accommodate extra-hour assignments may reflect the family unit's assessment of its ability to meet both its financial and its care-providing goals. The facilities for providing required care-giving responsibilities are more 'built in' (that is, partners not working or working less than full-time) for the UK male respondent, whereas the UK female respondent must look outside the household for assistance with care-provision responsibilities. The greater and more evenly matched ability of US females and US males

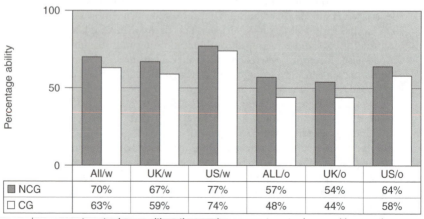

	All/w	UK/w	US/w	ALL/o	UK/o	US/o
■ NCG	70%	67%	77%	57%	54%	64%
□ CG	63%	59%	74%	48%	44%	58%

/w = accepts extra hours with notice   /o = accepts extra hours without notice

Figure 6.3 Accepting extra-hour assignments – non-wcare-givers vs. care-givers.

to perform extra-hour assignments, with and without notice, may indicate a greater satisfaction or acceptance of arrangements the respondent has in place for meeting the family unit's financial and care-providing goals. Rodgers and Rodgers' (1989) findings seem pertinent: one study shows that two-thirds of the women under 40 who have reached the top echelons in our largest companies and institutions are childless, whilst virtually all men in leadership positions are fathers.

Availability of dependant-care arrangements

The ability of care-givers to expand their working hours (with and without prior notice) appears for some to be connected to their ability to obtain appropriate and reliable additional care for their dependants. (For others, the ability to obtain extra-hour coverage does not seem to be a factor. Many respondents disclosed either a change in career objective after having children or that they simply felt that they no longer had the energy or will to pursue their careers aggressively at this stage in their lives.) For those requiring additional care-giving coverage, the ready availability of that coverage was vital. Figure 6.4 reveals the use of paid care facilities by UK and US child-care-givers.

The participating banks had little or no involvement with their employees in the provision or remuneration of care facilities. All respondents indicated that care-giving facilities were self-provided.

The alternatives for securing dependant-care coverage generally required either payment for the services or the services being provided 'free' – that is, without expenditure of currency. Barter arrangements are not unknown. If 'free', family, friends and/or neighbours are generally involved in the acceptable arrangements.

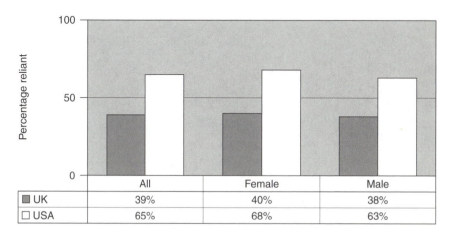

	All	Female	Male
■ UK	39%	40%	38%
□ USA	65%	68%	63%

Figure 6.4 Care-giver employees using paid care-provider facilities.

Several written comments volunteered in the UK survey disclosed some concern about the availability of child-care facilities. Several wrote that their employer should provide on-site care. One worried about her career and her future: 'Should I choose to start a family in the future, I am concerned about the level of child care available and how this would suit my work pattern.' Another may have spoken for many: 'I am happy with my career development but only as I have excellent support from my family who look after my children while I am working. But this (career) may have been more difficult if that support was not available. I know other employees who are not so lucky.'

UK care-givers relied heavily on obtaining unpaid dependant-care services (61 per cent) while US care-givers relied just as heavily on paid dependant-care services (65 per cent). Surprisingly, given the very large advantage that UK males have with 'built in' care-providers (that is, stay-at-home partners or partners working part time), there was similarity between UK females and UK males in reliance on paid care-provider facilities. Sixty-eight per cent of US female care-giver respondents relied on paid services while only 40 per cent of UK female care-giver respondents did. The differences are statistically significant in both categories. This finding begs the questions of availability, of choice and of adequacy.

Dorothy is 30 years of age, spent 2 years at college, has been employed for 8 years, works full time, is married and her partner works full time. She is expecting her first child, has been promoted twice and is currently a Senior Systems Analyst II. She confides: 'While I am not affected by child care at present, I will be in the near future. I am conscious that career opportunities may be limited if I wish to devote more time to caring for my child at home; whereas, if a crèche facility was provided at work I could overcome this and continue my career development.'

Jones and Causer (1995) apparently speak for many researchers when they cite numerous studies that have identified potential motherhood and motherhood as 'impacting detrimentally' on women's opportunities for employment and promotion. They allege that the typical male employee's family commitments impinge marginally, if at all, on work responsibilities. In conclusion these data show that care-givers (those employees with family responsibilities – male employees as well as female employees; with elder dependants as well as children) are not as available for working as and when required by their employer as are non-care-givers. This is similar in both the USA and the UK. However, those in the UK rely more upon family and friends to provide cover, whilst those in the USA rely more upon paid help. In both countries the banking organisations studied do not generally provide facilities for care-giving, although some of the respondents felt that they should do so.

7 Care-giving and development opportunities

This chapter examines the disparity of development opportunities made available to care-givers and non-care-givers, and the impact this has upon the career of care-givers, whether male of female. Do employees identified as care-givers receive different amounts of career-development opportunities than employees identified as non-care-givers? This question has parallels with the literature on in-house development in Chapter 2. Recall that human capital theory argues that wages were not determined by productivity alone but also by the cash returns to workers who had invested in increasing their work-related skills, and that 'human capital' referred to the knowledge workers acquired through the investment of time and money to become more productive. Further, 'Human Capital theory argues that women are more likely than men to quit their jobs prematurely. Because of this, firms are reluctant to hire them for positions that involve employer-financed training . . . jobs that involve high levels of firm-specific skills' (Cohn, 1996).

Natalie is 38 years old, has a Masters degree, is married and works part time as a Customer Service clerk (22.5 hours per week, with an additional 5 hours per week spent travelling to and from work). Her partner works full time. They have one child, of grade-school age, and Natalie is the principal care-giver. She estimates that she earns 20 per cent of the household income. She accepts assignments outside of normal work hours with notice most of the time and without notice occasionally. Natalie slightly disagrees that her employer supports and understands her care-giving responsibilities and is neutral on invoking the care-giving policies that are in place. Natalie said: 'No specific career development or training is offered when you work reduced hours. There is an assumption that you are *less* committed'.

The expectation would be that the surveyed banks would select employees to receive management training and development who are perceived to have both the requisite ability and 'commitment' to the bank. No data were collected that could be interpreted as reflecting the bank's judgement with reference to the ability of any employee. Data were collected that allowed the surveyed population to be segmented into groups that reflected whether employees were (or were not) with family responsibilities. Evidence for examining this proposition includes comparative data supplied by the survey respondents in the areas of: participation in formal development programmes; management development training; mentors appointed; performance-appraisal reviews; receipt of specific career advice during formal performance-appraisal reviews; and development goals reduced to writing and followed up.

Formalised career-development programme

Figure 7.1 depicts the participation in formal development programmes of non-care-givers as compared to the care-givers in total and by country. Non-care-givers were included significantly more often. UK male respondents enjoyed the advantage of being included in formal career-development plans more frequently than UK females. In the USA, no statistically significant differences arose between the females and males on inclusion in formal career-development plans. Non-care-givers were included in formal career-development plans more frequently than care-givers, especially in the UK. No statistically significant differences between the UK and the USA or between females and males were found in the presence or absence of formal career-development plans within care-giver or non-care-giver categories.

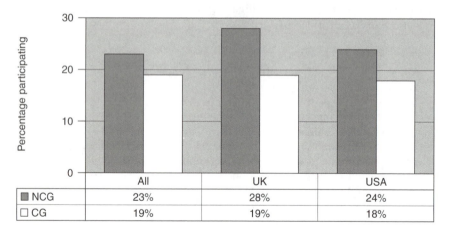

	All	UK	USA
■ NCG	23%	28%	24%
□ CG	19%	19%	18%

Figure 7.1 Care-giver/non-care-giver participation in formal development programmes.

Career-development (management) training

Banks in both countries seem to provide about the same amount of management-training opportunity for their respondents and disburse it without regard to gender. However, as is indicated in Figure 7.2, analysis by care-giving status revealed a statistically significant preference for providing training to those employees *without* care-giver responsibilities.

Within the care-giver category itself, UK banks provided management training to the male more frequently than to the female, whilst no significant differences were found when comparing management training given to US female and male care-givers. It is possible to speculate that the UK male/female differences in hours worked, ability to work extra-hour assignments, and alternatives available for satisfying the family unit's financial and care-provision goals may be factors in these results.

Harriett is 27 years old, has a high school/secondary school education, works full time (40 hours a week with 5 hours a week travel time), has one 4-year-old child and is expecting her second child in a few months. She is married and her partner works full time. Harriett earns 25 per cent of the household income. She has had some in-house career-development training that she sought and received. Harriett had this to say: 'I have a 4-year-old son and I am expecting another baby in a few months. I have always put my family before education. Therefore, I have not the time to enrol in additional training courses to be able to be promoted within the company.'

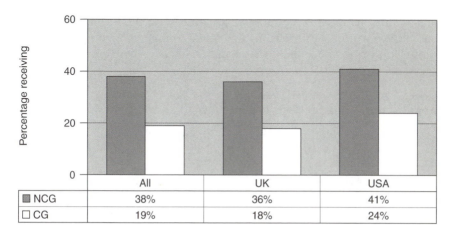

	All	UK	USA
■ NCG	38%	36%	41%
□ CG	19%	18%	24%

Figure 7.2 Receipt of management training – care-givers vs. non-care-givers.

Perceptions of commitment and of the employees' ability to contribute to corporate goals might influence evaluations of suitability for management training. This might explain why care-givers received less management training, but fails to explain why UK female non-care-givers also received significantly less management training. More specific research is needed to identify the reasons why UK male respondents have received management-training opportunities more frequently than UK female respondents, and this might be one area in which the glass ceiling is, indeed, gendered.

Specifically appointed mentors

The analysis of survey responses to the question of having had a mentor formally appointed to assist with career development showed no statistically significant differences between or within the UK and the USA, females and males or care-givers and non-care-givers. Approximately 20 per cent of UK and US respondents reported having (or having had) mentors. Yet most of the banks describe the mentoring efforts as a work in progress and are implementing it on a more or less informal basis. Although not statistically significant, it may be of some directional assistance to note that the breakdown of mentoring in the UK was reported as 26 per cent of female respondents and 18 per cent of male respondents. Twenty per cent of the US female respondents and 14 per cent of the US male respondents reported having or having had mentors. This finding is at variance with some of the literature. Flynn (1996) reported that lack of mentoring was specifically noted by women as a reason for slow progress by females.

From the responses to this question, it appears that the use of formal mentors is rather a young but growing trend. The replies from the respondents appear to be referring to a combination of old-style informal and new-style formal mentoring rather than addressing the formal mentoring question as written. A review of the written comments accompanying the survey indicated anecdotally that females seem to desire and be more aggressive in pursuit of mentoring than males.

Regular performance-appraisal reviews

Performance-appraisal programmes were a uniform feature of all the banks surveyed. Over 90 per cent of all respondents surveyed indicated that they regularly received performance appraisals. By and large, the reporting banks in both countries seem to insist that performance appraisals be carried out periodically and by the immediate supervisor. No difference in receipt of performance appraisals was noted in any category of the surveyed population. The respondents' views of the effectiveness of the follow-up action referenced in the appraisal varied from bank to bank.

Comments were sketchy, and not particularly suited to statistical procedure. There were no indications in the respondents' remarks that any one in any of the segments under study was treated disproportionately.

Receiving specific career-development advice and counsel during formal performance-appraisal reviews

Specific career-development advice was received during formal performance-appraisal discussions by 48 per cent of the UK respondents and 49 per cent of the US respondents. No statistically significant differences were detected between the UK and the USA, females and males or care-givers and non-care-givers in regards to the question. Overall, there is some indication that the UK banks provide this guidance somewhat more frequently than the US banks, but this trend is not confirmed in any of the other segmentations.

Reducing career goals to writing

The UK banks followed the practice of making a written record of the goals agreed between the employee and the supervisor more frequently than occurred in the USA, for both male and female segments. More emphasis on written goal-setting was accorded the non-care-giver respondents than the care-givers respondents in both the UK and USA, particularly in the USA.

The UK participating banks appear to have more formalised procedures for implementing their performance appraisal/goal-setting process and the majority of respondents rated these procedures as effective. Although pursuing performance appraisal with similar vigour, the USA does not appear to formalise the process to the extent of the UK participating banks.

In summary, to a degree that is statistically significant, non-care-giver respondents were more frequently enrolled in formal career-development programmes, more frequently received management training and more frequently had written career goals than care-giver respondents. Virtually all respondents received annual performance appraisals and about half received specific career advice during these appraisals. Since performance appraisals are more of a corporate employee-evaluation device than an employee-development device, uniform application of the procedure across all lines and categories of employees is to be expected. Only one of the banks had a formal mentoring-programme policy in a work-in-process state. Some others were attempting to install the practice on an informal basis. As such, the mentoring programmes were too new to evaluate.

The key areas for tracking career development are participation in formal career-development programmes and receipt of management training (both in-house and outside management-development training, including participation in formal higher-education programmes). In both of these areas the evidence is that care-givers were not accorded the same degree of career-development opportunity as non-care-givers. The evidence shows that firms are more reluctant to invest in employer-financed training and development activities for either females or males with distracting care-giving responsibilities than they are for those without such responsibilities, in both the USA and the UK.

8 Care-giving and career attainment

This chapter examines the careers of care-givers across organisational levels, and finds that care-giving is a glass ceiling and that it is not gender specific. If care-givers showed less 'commitment' (fewer hours on the job and not as available for extra-hour work) and participated in fewer career-development activities, then the expectation is that care-givers would not be able to achieve a similar degree of job advancement within their employment hierarchy to that achieved by the non-care-givers. Job information was consolidated into four general job-grade positions: clerical/hourly; junior management/technical/supervisor; manager (departmental); executive (officer of the organisation).

Review of statistical evidence

No statistically significant differences were detected between the job-level attainment of UK banking respondents and US banking respondents, nor did such differences emerge when comparing UK and US female-respondent accomplishment or UK and US male-respondent accomplishment. However, uniformly across all cross-cultural categories (all females versus all males, UK females versus UK males, US females versus US males), males recorded higher job-level achievement than females. The predominance of males achieving higher-level positions that was revealed in the overall female/male comparisons continued in the within-category comparisons. Within the UK, males respondents achieved higher-level positions more frequently than female respondents within both non-care-giver and care-giver comparisons. The same occurred in the USA.

Job-level-attainment comparison of non-care-giver respondents and care-giver respondents

In order to make a comparison of the relative career progress of the categories to be compared, the data were segmented on the following bases:

non-care-givers – defined as those respondents without care-giving responsibilities (neither dependent children under 18 years of age nor elders living within the same household) without regard to the employment status of their partners;

care-givers – defined as those respondents with care-giving responsibilities without regard to the employment status of their partners, if any.

Figure 8.1 depicts the comparison of job-level attainment as defined for this segmentation of data.

In six of the seven categories compared, a statistically significant difference was present. There was little uniformity in the differences between the care-giver and non-care-giver categories overall, but different female/male tendencies do appear to be present. In total (UK and USA) care-giver respondents have a stronger presence in the executive level (Level 4) than do non-care-giver respondents, with the situation reversing itself at the next two lower levels. Non-care-giver respondents dominate Levels 2 (supervisory) and 3 (managerial). On the whole, female non-care-giver respondents (both USA and UK) appear to reach the supervisory and managerial levels more frequently than do female care-giver respondents.

Females present at the executive level were too few in number to place reliance on a trend that favours either group. Males at the executive level of both UK and US banks predominantly come from the care-giver category, though more so in the UK than the USA. The trend runs counter to the demographics of the 'up and coming' future managers currently inhabiting Level 2 and much of Level 3. Further research effort is needed to explain these incongruous results. On the face of it, job-level attain-

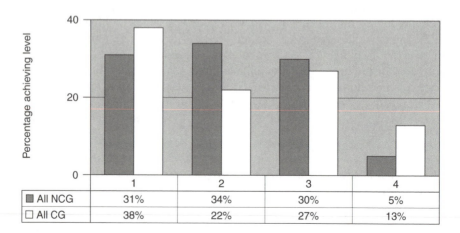

Figure 8.1 Job-level attainment by position grade – total survey.

ment at senior level would appear to be independent of care-giver or non-care-giver status. This raises the question of just who within the family is shouldering those daily care-providing responsibilities – employee, spouse (partner) or both. The high proportion of Levels 3 and 4 care-giver male manager respondents with non-gainfully or part-time employed partners (70 per cent and 75 per cent respectively in the UK, for example) may be influencing this counter-intuitive presence of care-giver respondents at the higher organisational levels. Possibly at the executive level, the 'traditional' family structure is alive and well.

Restatement of the job-level-attainment question

None of the literature reviewed for this book examined the issue of career progression through the individuals' organisational ladder. However, the literature does address the notion that career paths can be inconsistent with the lifestyle of a person with serious family responsibilities (Rodgers and Rodgers, 1989). The anecdotal evidence compiled from the survey is replete with 'family comes first' sentiments, especially from those who could be considered the primary care-provider for the daily needs of the family. Care-givers are supposed to have less ability to show 'commitment' than non-care-givers. Empirical evidence that care-giver respondents are predominant in the executive suite runs counter to the evidence presented previously that non-care-giver respondents are able to work longer hours, are more available for extra hours with and without notice, and receive more training and development. Does the finding that at the higher levels of employment care-giver respondents are achieving the same job levels as non-care-giver respondents mean that any differences in hours worked, extra-hour availability, receipt of lesser training and so on does not matter since the job progress for both groups is the same? Or does it mean that there is a need to search further for any common ground that may exist between some care-givers and non-care-givers? We need to look again at our definition of care-givers and non-care-givers and look further at the qualitative data from the executive interviews.

Care-giving and work status of spouse (partner)

In order to make meaningful comparisons of the relative career progress of those with and without the responsibility for the primary daily care provision for their family, the data was re-segmented on the following basis:

non-care-givers – defined as those respondents without care-giving responsibilities (neither dependent children nor elders living within the same household) **plus** those care-givers whose partners were either not gainfully employed (NGE) or worked only part time;

> **care-givers** – defined as those respondents with care-giving responsibilities whose partners worked full time **plus** respondents with care-giving responsibilities who were without partners (single, divorced, separated or widowed).

Such a re-segmentation of data recognises the reality of the additional freedom to pursue career enjoyed by respondents whose partners are at home full time or part time. It reflects the presumption that the family unit has decided that one member will primarily be responsible for maximising the financial rewards and that the other partner will primarily be responsible for maximising the care-provision rewards. The essential delineation posed by this comparison is: 'Is home-base covered?' – in other words, are the employee's care-giving responsibilities, if any, being attended to by the partner while the employee is at work, thus endowing the employee with 'time-freedom' to pursue career objectives (should that be the employee's desire)?

Daniel has a BSc degree and is a chartered accountant. He has worked for his firm for more than 20 years, is married and has two grown children. His partner does charity work and owns a counselling business. However, while the children were growing up, she stayed home and took the lion's share of the child-care responsibilities so that Daniel could pursue his career to the fullest. He said: 'Having children was not a negative, but a plus in my career. However, had I not been in a stable marriage, this could have changed and care-giving could have become a negative.'

Combining the job-level accomplishments of non-care-giver respondents with the accomplishments of care-giver respondents with non-gainfully employed partners and part-time employed partners reinforced the advantage this group held over care-giver respondents with full-time working partners at all levels above entry level (Level 1). The dominance at the supervisory and managerial job levels (Levels 2 and 3) grew whilst the prior dominance of care-giver respondents with full-time working partners over non-care-giver respondents at the executive level (Level 4) was reversed. The differences between the compared groups of respondents were statistically significant. Figure 8.2 reflects these results.

Examination of the care-giver respondent group by itself revealed that for the whole UK/US sample, a statistically significant difference was exhibited between the job-level accomplishments of those care-giver respondents whose partners were either not gainfully employed or were employed only part time as compared with those care-giver respondents whose partners worked full time or were without partners. This same, significantly different, pattern holds true for both the UK and the US samples, when taken separately. Figure 8.3 depicts these results.

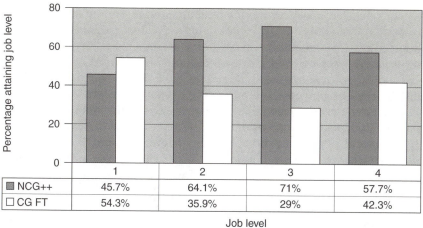

	1	2	3	4
■ NCG++	45.7%	64.1%	71%	57.7%
□ CG FT	54.3%	35.9%	29%	42.3%

Job level
NCG++ = Partner not gainfully employed + CG = Part-time employed
CG FT = Full-time employed or no partner

Figure 8.2 Job-level attainment by partner's employment status – total survey.

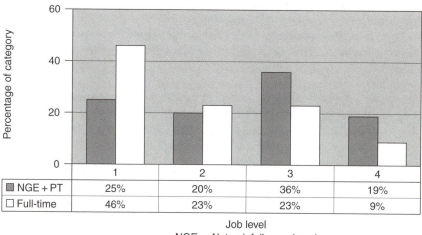

	1	2	3	4
■ NGE + PT	25%	20%	36%	19%
□ Full-time	46%	23%	23%	9%

Job level
NGE = Not gainfully employed
PT = Part-time employed
Full-time = Full-time employed

Figure 8.3 Job level of employee and partner's employment status – care-givers (only), total survey.

Family-unit arrangements – male and female

A more detailed review of the job-level attainment of only the care-giver-respondent category within each country revealed a marked difference between the females and the males in the arrangements each gender had in place for securing what it saw as the optimum balance between financial and care-provision rewards. Figures 8.4, 8.5, 8.6 and 8.7 illustrate these differences – by gender – within both the UK and the USA.

UK female care-giver respondents reported having full-time working partners the great majority of the time – 75 per cent at the executive level (Level 4) and 89 per cent and above for job levels 1, 2 and 3. The opposite occurred with UK male respondents – 75 per cent of executives (Level 4) had non-gainfully employed or part-time employed partners with the number increasing as the job responsibility increased – 57 per cent at clerical level, 65 per cent at supervisory level and 74 per cent at managerial level, respectively.

Similarly, US female care-giver respondents reported having full-time working partners the great majority of the time – 100 per cent at the executive level (only five reporting, however) and 72 per cent to 80 per cent for job levels 1, 2 and 3. As with the UK, the opposite occurs with US male care-giver respondents – 60 per cent of executives had non-gainfully employed or part-time employed partners with a range of 66–72 per cent for clerical, supervisory and managerial levels.

Most female respondents with care-giving responsibilities had full-time working partners. This held true at all job levels within the participating

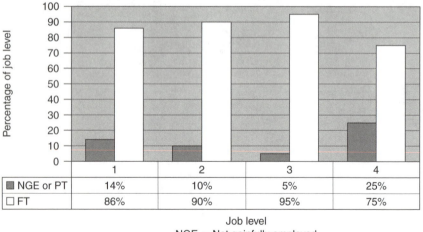

	1	2	3	4
■ NGE or PT	14%	10%	5%	25%
□ FT	86%	90%	95%	75%

Job level
NGE = Not gainfully employed
PT = Part-time employed
FT = Full-time employed or no partner

Figure 8.4 UK female care-givers by job level and partner's employment status.

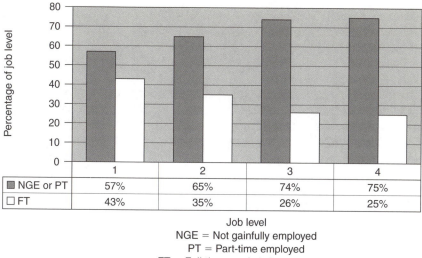

Job level
NGE = Not gainfully employed
PT = Part-time employed
FT = Full-time employed or no partner

Figure 8.5 UK male care-givers by job level and partner's employment status.

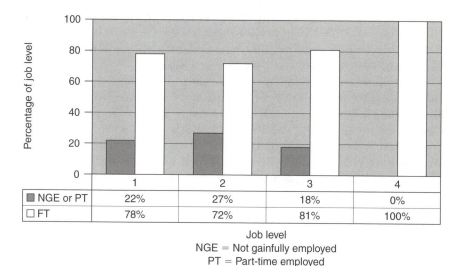

Job level
NGE = Not gainfully employed
PT = Part-time employed
FT = Full-time employed or no partner

Figure 8.6 US female care-givers by job level and partner's employment status.

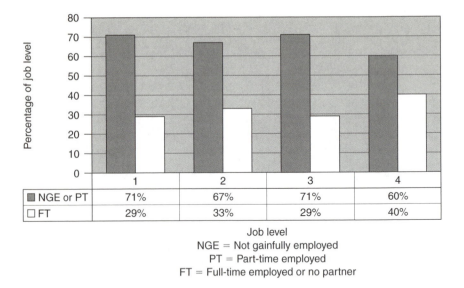

	1	2	3	4
■ NGE or PT	71%	67%	71%	60%
□ FT	29%	33%	29%	40%

Job level
NGE = Not gainfully employed
PT = Part-time employed
FT = Full-time employed or no partner

Figure 8.7 US male care-givers by job level and partner's employment status.

organisations. The opposite was found for male respondents with care-giving responsibilities. Most male care-giver respondents had partners who were either not gainfully employed or who worked only part-time. It is pertinent to recall that male care-giver respondents were more frequently in higher job-level positions than females care-givers.

The evidence suggests than the relationship between job-level attainment and partner's employment status is not independent in any of the three compared combinations – UK/USA, UK alone and USA alone. These findings are in line with those of Rodgers and Rodgers (1989), who reported that two-thirds of women under 40 who have reached the executive level are childless while virtually all men in leadership positions are fathers, and echo a dominant refrain of the literature – insurmountable social and economic barriers are put in the way of those who want both a career and a family (Moore, 1996). The tension between family and career is discussed further in the next chapter.

9   Care-giving and time/freedom: is home-base covered?

This chapter addresses points raised in the earlier chapters in this part of the book to conclude that the effects of care-giving vary and are linked directly to the extent to which care-givers have the home-base covered – in other words, those that have adequate and prompt support for their dependants are better able to progress in their careers, whether male or female.

The dictatorship of time

'There are only so many hours in a day' is an expression familiar to all. Since childhood we have continually been reminded of it. Technology lets us occasionally play with the exceptions – we can jet to and fro between the time zones and stretch 'today' into 30 hours or longer; computer technology has eased the burden of record keeping, paperwork and communications (amongst many other things); and household chores have been fundamentally altered over the last half-century – but the yesteryear song that lamented 'What a difference a day makes, 24 little hours' still holds true.

It could be said that technological progress has lessened the time required for the daily essentials of sleep, food, shelter and so on and has increased the time available for the pursuit of personal dreams. However, some of these dreams have become today's essentials. For some, time taken for the care and development of children has increased with societal pressure from the days when children took adult roles early in life and 'raised themselves'. For others, the increasing predominance of the nuclear (rather than extended) family in the Western world has meant that care of elderly parents and others now falls on fewer shoulders. Still others – the majority that is either no longer encumbered by care-giving concerns or has never assumed such encumbrance – have their own important dreams to pursue within the limited time available – dreams which, because of the accessibility of communications and the development of the media culture, are becoming ever more central to the 'wannabe' society.

Work–life issues centre around the desire or need for employees to have more time off from work to attend to personal issues. Such issues are not confined to care-giving and can broadly be equated with anything not connected to the job that is causing increase in the stress levels of the employees. However, for the purposes of this book, the focus remains on work–life issues arising from employee care-giving responsibilities. At the core of work–life issues is time and resource (self). The tension is between the time required to discharge care-giving responsibilities in a manner that satisfies the minimum level of the self-established priority for care-giving and the time commitment required to earn the resources necessary to satisfy the minimum level of the self-established priority for life.

We have cited some evidence of the trends showing increasing hours being worked by all employees, increasing participation of mothers in the workforce, increasing concerns of care-givers that family must come first, increasing concerns of 'necessity' that impel many to work, and the near unanimous perception that long hours are necessary in order to be seen to merit the promotions that (are presumed to) increase the rewards for time spent at work. This raises the question of time – and its dictatorship over our lives. As Galinsky, Bond and Friedman (1993) summarised, the 'time bind' created by the simultaneous rise in family and work procedures has been evident for several years and appears to be getting worse.

Career or family?

Every society and all individuals within society have had to address the question of how to care for dependants, particularly children and the elderly population; however, this is not just a social problem. Individuals, organisations and societies have to balance the social mores with economic sustainability and income generation. Essentially, care-giving costs money. It removes from the potential workforce those who otherwise, in whole or in part, could be generating income, which reduces the income-generation ability of those requiring care-giving services. It can generate income for those who provide care-giving services, which translates into costs for those who need the services. When not supplied as needed, the attendant social problems of not having provided the care also accrue costs, some of which can be long term.

Some make the choice between career and family early on in their lives, but the choice is neither simple nor inviolate. Individual and family circumstances change, as do company benefits and national policies. For example, care for dependants can arise in an unexpected fashion, and even if it were possible to make such a decision based upon financial criteria (thereby ignoring such things as job satisfaction), the emotional issues associated with the decision can be numerous. In many cases, therefore, we suggest that the 'choice' is a matter of circumstance and that a clear rational decision between career or family is a rarity.

Christopher and Maureen are high-flyers, married, he works in the legal department as a Senior Legal Advisor, working 42 hours a week plus having 2 hours' weekly commuting time to and from work, she works as a Senior Personnel Manager, working 42 hours a week plus having 2 hours weekly commuting time as well. Christopher has been with the firm for 12 years and Maureen for 10 years. They have both been promoted a number of times. When first married, they worked in separate locations and had a long-distance marriage. Five years ago, they both were transferred to the home office and for the first time commute to work together. They delayed having children to pursue their careers. Two years ago Christopher's parents were in an automobile accident, which left his father paralysed from the waist down. His mother suffered a heart attack 6 months ago and can no longer lift and care for his father. Following the heart attack, Christopher's parents came to live with Christopher and Maureen. Maureen's parents are elderly, have some health issues and have lived with Maureen and Christopher since they got married. The couple shared their thoughts on how they are coping: 'We never really planned to have all of our parents depending on us. We delayed having children so that we could concentrate on both our careers. Now this. We will cope the best we can and make decisions as necessary about who will take the primary role of care-giver. We currently have someone providing hot meals for them 5 days a week and a bath and phys-ical therapy for Chris's father weekly. That has been a big help. We have tried to stagger time off needed to take them to doctor appointments, etc. We just cope daily. We have some policies in place that will allow us some flexibility in how we work. We have good salaries to live comfortably and we both love our work. The problem is we don't know how this will affect our careers or our ability to have our own family.'

The central question therefore becomes 'Is home-base covered?'. 'Home-base' is used here as a pseudonym for the responsibilities associated with home and family life. If the employee has home-base covered, then the employee's care-giving responsibilities, if any, are primarily being attended to by someone else, and the employee's available time is extended in its relationship with resources and priorities. The empirical evidence revealed that those employees who had home-base covered (defined here as employees who had partners not gainfully employed or part-time employed or employees who were without care-giving responsibilities) attained higher career positions more frequently than those employees who didn't have home-base covered (employees with care-giving responsibilities who have partners that work full time or single employees with care-giving responsibilities). Many respondents com-mented that their care-giving responsibilities had curtailed their ability to render the perceived requirement of long hours. On the other hand, a number of these comments made it explicit that some people rejected the assumption that they wanted additional career responsibilities, especially after they had willingly taken on family responsibilities. This echoes Yoest's comment that 'you have this whole movement saying intelligent women shouldn't spend their time this way (at home). It is emptying motherhood of all social content' (Wilson, 1996).

The qualitative evidence obtained from the executive interviews helps provide an explanation for the quantitative identification of the phenomenon and illustrates the freedom to pursue career provided by having home-base covered. Relative freedom to pursue career becomes *the* defining factor of the care-giving/career-progression debate. How well home-base is covered establishes the parameters within which the alternatives for utilising time and resources are examined and priorities are established.

Class and gender

The balance between care-giving and career progression changes in nature at different levels of the organisation. The previous chapter showed that female executives more frequently had home dependants than males and more frequently had working partners than males. Although some of the female executives worked part time, none of the male executives did. Clearly, therefore, care-giving does not hinder career progression at this level.

Burton (1985) maintained that differences between women of different classes are more significant than their common gender identity. Similarly, Billings and Alvesson (1992) stated their belief that there are clear social class differences between women in terms of orientations to work and that these differences may be greater than gender differences. The term 'class' itself may be taking on different meanings and/or be manifested in non-conventional ways. Taylor (1997) notes that there are many things that act as social class signifiers, including occupation type, level of education, speech and dialect, body language, manner of dress, spatial locality and type of housing. She concludes that determining membership of a specific social class also has much to do with the labels attached to people by those in power. In the USA, 'class' is generally associated with money (with monetary ranges frequently quoted for each of the class subdivisions) or occupation (denoted by 'white collar' or 'blue collar'). The UK is perceived as taking a more 'traditional' view of class – 'old' money or past/present family position being considered as having a bearing upon class subdivisions; however, the Americanisation of the corporate environment (Boyacigiller and Adler, 1991) suggests that relative wealth be considered as 'class' for the purposes of this book.

Those holding a superior position in an organisation, therefore, could be considered to be in a higher class – by virtue of receiving higher pay – than those in subordinate positions. We might assume that those with higher pay have a greater disposable income, and thus seek different solutions to the care-giving dilemma than do those with less money available to spend on it. This notion supports some of the difference in response elicited from the survey and the executive interviews. For example, some survey respondents called for crèches to alleviate long-hour or unexpected-extra-hour demand stress, whereas a female executive asserted that employees would rather select their own care-provider.

Those receiving higher pay may be better positioned to pay for care-providers, whereas in-house crèches may be more favoured by the lesser paid. Mobility may also be associated with class. Those who seek the better positions are frequently required to relocate to another area to achieve a better position. Relocation frequently removes the employee from near-ness to family relatives. Those care-givers without relatives may have little choice but to use paid care-providers whereas those who are not so mobile and have remained in the family neighbourhood may find the family to be the care-provider of choice. Such differences call into question the wisdom of applying the same policies across all levels of the organisation.

The view of the organisation

The executives were asked their views on how their organisation could better handle work–life issues. They showed recognition and some sympathy for work–life-balance problems and acknowledgement of the need for the banks to be competitive (both commercially and HR-policy-wise). One executive described his vision of the bank's future approach: 'We should embrace part-time and embrace home working and anything else that would allow us to have good people working on our books whether it be some part of the day or some part of the week.'

As an interesting aside it is worth noting that males and females responded on two different levels. The males, particularly in the USA, adopted a structured organisational perspective. They replied in terms of what the organisation would or could do and did not elaborate from their own personal view. The two single US females also answered in this fashion. In contrast, the females and, to a certain extent, the UK males answered more from a personal point of view or in terms of their own situation. This difference in focus of response is not entirely gendered, nor can it be accounted for entirely by national difference. By this we mean that one might expect US individualism and its correlate of assuming personal rather than societal support for care-giving to result in a focus upon organisational structures when considering what might be changed. Similarly, one might expect that the UK's more communitarian approach to this could lead to a focus upon individual need. Perhaps this is an area for further research.

In summary: four overarching themes

There were four overarching care-giving themes that emerged from the qualitative data and also from the comments of the surveyed employees.

These themes cut across level of employment, income, gender and nationality. These four themes are summarised below.

Long hours

Employers regarded employees who worked long hours (come early, stay late) as displaying prima-facie evidence of commitment to the firm and to the job. This theme ran through all the empirical data.

Part-time work

Part-time employees received lesser training and were not considered as having promotion potential. Taken in conjunction with the theme of long hours, the part-time employees were considered by some to be 'less committed'. This was evident in the survey responses as well as the interviews.

'Family comes first'

This theme ties both long hours and part-time work to the care-giving responsibilities and the priorities established by care-giver employees. The survey comments showed that those with care-giving responsibilities nearly all placed their duty to their dependants first, and their career second.

Work–life issues

This theme, the need to find balance between the demands of work and the individuals' responsibilities to themselves and others, was evident in all the empirical data. The comments and perceptions of the interviewed executives evidence a recognition of the work–life tensions ('family more priority than almighty dollar'), recognition of 'need work–life balance' and the need to 'not work less but more flexibly'. Yet the executives remind that 'the business of the bank must get done'.

The four main themes from this research – long hours, part-time work, family comes first and work–life issues – helped collate the many strands of thought around care-giving. Whilst none of the four themes may be said to lay bare the root cause(s) of the adverse effects of care-giving upon career development/progression, the comments of the respondents add depth to the understanding of the tensions and the dilemmas posed thereby. The defining factor of 'freedom to pursue career' provides the framework for analysing the tension between time and resources. These tensions and dilemmas affect, either directly or indirectly, all parts of society, from the individual, the organisation and the State to the policy makers. They are addressed explicitly in the final part of this book.

Part III

Implications

Part I of this book examined the literature around care-giving and career progression and suggested that whilst there was a plethora of facts, figures and opinions in this area, there was little that arose directly from the area, and that those figures that did arise from the area were rarely comparable. In other words, it raised the need for empirical evidence.

Part II accepted that challenge and presented empirical evidence from several studies (directly comparing the UK and the USA) that showed that care-giving could be seen as a gender neutral glass ceiling. In general, care-givers are seen to be less committed to their work and receive less training and development opportunities, and are seen as less suitable for promotion. This occurs whether they work part time or full time. Some care-givers, however, do not face these problems, and it is they who 'have home-base covered'.

In essence, Part III examines the issue of 'is home-base covered?'. The first chapter in this part looks at the wider issues of an ageing population and the need for organisations and society to retain their pool of experience buried (and often unused and unrecognised) in the care-givers. The following three chapters revisit the wider debate informed by the empirical evidence presented in Parts I and II, and examine key issues and the implications these findings have for the different sectors of society (individual, organisation and State). The part, and the book, concludes with outlines of further research needed and some policy-related remarks.

10 Emerging issues

In this chapter two key emerging issues are examined – the demographic changes overtaking the world and the disconnections that are being experienced by many employees and want-to-be employees between their lives and their work.

Moen and Yu (2000) comment that very few contemporary workers have the time, opportunity or inclination to devote themselves exclusively to their paid work. As a result, families develop strategies to reduce the family-demand side of the work–family equation. Two such strategies that have been adopted culture-wide are: (1) postponing marriage and/or childbearing; and (2) reducing family size. The rising number of nannies and *au pairs* points to another strategy for those who can afford it, that is 'hiring' a wife. These strategies, whilst made at the individual level, collectively impact upon the future of the State. The first two strategies are of particular importance here as they point to the collapsing birth-rate that is now being identified in many countries.

Changing demographics of Western society

> In 1950, worldwide the average woman had five children. Today she has just 2.7, and the continued collapse of fertility is set to become the dominant demographic feature of the 21st century. . . . New UN population forecasts . . . conclude that within two generations four out of five of the world's women will be having two children or fewer.
>
> (Pearce, 2002)

The 1998 projection for the population of the world in 2150 was nearly 10 billion, but 2002 figures have revised that estimate, such that in the best-case scenario (as of Sweden – see below) it will be just over 5 billion, and thus below our current population of 6 billion, and in the worst-case scenario it will drop to just over 3 billion (as of Italy).

It takes an average of 2.1 children per woman of childbearing age to maintain the population at a constant level. The European Union has an average live-birth-rate of approximately 1.48 and Japan is hovering around

Lisa is 37 years of age, has a high school/secondary education, is a non-care-giver and works full time. She is married and her partner also works full time. They share household earnings 50/50. They have no dependants. In her position as Junior Management Project Manager she works 35 hours per week and travels an additional 4 hours to and from work. She has a mentor. Her immediate supervisor does her performance appraisals and specific career advice is being given. She has written goals and objectives and almost always accepts assignments outside of normal working hours with notice and frequently accepts those without notice. She said that she personally has not experienced any effects from care-giving policies giving time off to others. Lisa had this to say: 'I feel I have a lot to give as I have chosen *not* to have children so I can pursue a career and opportunities.'

a 1.3 birth-rate. The USA at a 2.1 birth-rate appears within reasonable sustainability of population until around 2010 when the birth-rate is expected to commence free fall. Drucker (1999) dramatically characterised the demographic situation of the developed world: 'Japan and all of Southern Europe – Portugal, Spain, Southern France, Italy, Greece – are drifting toward collective national suicide by the end of the 21st century'. He calculated that by the end of the twenty-first century, Italy, with a present population of 60 million, might be down to 20–21 million; Japan – at 125 million presently – might be down to 50–55 million.

According to Pearce (2002) this dramatic drop in birth-rate is not the result of disease or poverty, religion or forced contraception. For example, Italy, with a strong Catholic population has a rate of 1.2, and in Iran, where the mullahs have declared their opposition to the international agenda for cutting birth-rates, fertility crashed from 5.5 in 1988 to 2.2 in 2000. Similarly, Bangladesh and Vietnam have rates of 3.3 and 2.3 respectively, despite their poverty. Even African populations such as Kenya have dropped from 8 to 3 over the last few decades. Indeed, the birth-rate in almost all the countries that Pearce reviews has fallen, apart from an unusual few. These are in two groups. Sweden has a rate of 1.6, which, although below replacement level, is not continuing to fall and remains stable. Other northern European countries such as Norway, Britain and Finland show a similar trend. In the second group some countries, such as Argentina and Uruguay (2.5 and 3), have remained stable for 50 years, and some Muslim states (Afghanistan, 6.9; Saudi Arabia, 6.1; and Pakistan, 5.5) are continuing to increase.

Pearce argues persuasively that these trends are linked to the cultural diffusion of ideas influencing care-giving and career progression:

> On the farm even young children are an asset, minding the animals and helping with the harvest. In cities it's a different story: kids are more likely to be a liability – in purely economic terms at least. When

they are young they need looking after full-time, and when they are older they need educating to get any sort of job. On top of that cultural changes have increasingly liberated women from the home and child-rearing. In poor countries with a traditional patriarchal society, the spread of TV has opened many women's eyes to a whole new world, and modern birth control methods have allowed them to turn those aspirations into reality. ... Not having children has become a statement of modernity and emancipation, and women are unlikely to give up their new freedom.

Pearce argues that countries, such as Sweden, that have managed to stabilise their birth-rates have done so because of their supportive child-care policies rather than because the women have different aspirations:

[A Swedish woman] is just as keen to pursue a career. The difference is that she has more chance of combining a career with motherhood. Her suitors, who are more likely to have set up home on their own before marriage, are better housetrained, and Nordic governments are better at helping couples juggle family and work. About half the jobs held by Swedish women are part-time, crèches are near universal and paid parental leave lasts for a year. All this is unheard of in Italy, where only 12% of paid women have part-time jobs, and in Eastern Europe, where fertility rates have plunged since the collapse of communism wrecked state-funded support services for families.

(Pearce, 2002)

If Pearce is right, and our population in 2150 will be somewhere between 3 and 5 billion, depending whether the Swedish or Italian model comes to the fore globally, then the decisions that are made now about how best to support those that care for dependants will have a long-term and fundamental effect upon humanity, as well as upon the future of each nation.

Drucker sees the response to the situation slightly differently:

The birth rate collapse has tremendous political and social implications that we cannot even guess at today. But it will surely also have tremendous economic and business implications. ... Major innovations in work and employment are therefore already needed in Europe and Japan. In the United States there may still be enough young people to postpone radical changes until around 2010. Yet in all likelihood the new employment relations are likely to be developed first in the United States, again because it has the most flexible and least restrictive labour markets and a tradition of experimentation by individual employers as well as by individual employees.

(Drucker, 1999: 48)

In other words, whereas Pearce looks to systems of support for the care of dependants to generate a stable society, Drucker looks to organisations and the market for the same thing. This difference highlights the different approaches adopted by the USA and the UK, and impacts upon policy making in this area. We shall return to this in later chapters; first, however, we shall take a closer look at projections for the two countries.

An upturn in the USA?

The US Bureau of Labor Statistics (2003) reports the year 2000 civilian labour force over the age of 16 as 140 million, and projects its growth to 157 million by 2010. In 2000, males made up 53.4 per cent of the labour force and females 46.6 per cent. Females are projected to have the faster rising employment rate and by 2010 the breakdown is expected to be 52.1 per cent male and 47.9 per cent female. Of note is the projected change in the age of the workforce. Whilst there is little difference in the 16–24-year-old representation in the workforce between 2000 and 2010, the participation of 25 to 54 years olds is expected to drop from the present 71 per cent to 67 per cent with those aged 55 and older taking up the slack as their participation rises from 13 per cent to 17 per cent.

Similarly, the US Census Bureau (1996) projected that the total number of families in 2003 would be approximately 73.5 million, of which 44.8 per cent would have children in the household under the age of 18. Of these households, 73.8 per cent would be headed by a married couple, 20.9 per cent by a female head of house and 5.3 per cent by a male head of house. The breakdown of single-parent households was projected to be 80 per cent female and 20 per cent male, indicating an increasing male presence here. Projecting out to 2010, families with children under the age of 18 were estimated to drop to 41.3 per cent, as married-couple households were seen as dropping to 71.8 per cent, with female heads of house increasing to 22.3 per cent and male to 5.9 per cent. The female/male breakdown of single-parent households changes slightly to 79 per cent female and 21 per cent male. Gerbman (2000) postulated that elder-care will hit critical mass in 2011, when the first wave of baby boomers turns 65.

These projections would appear to confirm that the majority of employees are without care-giving responsibilities and that this majority status is expected to widen. 'The most common type of household after 2005 will be comprised of single persons and married couples without children' (Poe, 2000). Women are working more across the board but the biggest increase has come from women married to high-earning husbands, and Worrell and Cooper (1999) reported that in the buoyant job market, the demands of 'Generation X' were changing. Forty per cent of high-flyers said they intended to leave their employer within 2 years. Only 7 per cent expected to stay more than 5 years.

UK projections

Large and Saunders (1995) reported that over the last decade (1984–93), the British labour force has grown by 1.3 million people and that 92 per cent of the net increase were women, many of whom worked part-time. Large and Saunders cite projections by the UK Government Actuary's Department that the working population will increase by 1.5 million between 1993 and 2006, compared with a rise of 1.9 million in the previous 13 years. Of the projected 1.5 million total rise in the labour force by 2006, 1.3 million will be women. Women are projected to make up 46 per cent of the UK labour force by 2006, compared to 44 per cent in 1993. The report concluded that for most age groups, the proportions of women in or seeking work are projected to rise slightly each year while the proportion of males is expected to fall slightly – the increase of women in the civilian labour force is expected to be about four times greater than the increase of men. The projected labour force is expected to be somewhat older in 2006 than in 1993, with the 35–44 age band taking over from the 25–34 age band as the largest group – both for men and women.

The report noted that the trend for women reflects a number of economic and social factors, such as the availability of part-time work and changes in social attitudes. Women born in the latter part of the 1900s 'have tended to have an underlying attachment to the labour force', whereas the tendency to earlier retirement has affected the trends for men.

Though both Europe and the USA are expected to experience a rise in the median age, the US projection of relatively more children suggests higher public financing requirements for education as well as more pressure for public financing of child-care activities. Europe's 'dependency costs' would appear to be more concentrated in the elder-care areas. By 2050, the European population over the age of 65 is projected to be equivalent to 60 per cent of its working-age population, whereas the US population over 65 years of age is projected to be 40 per cent of its working-age population.

Migrant population

The US 2000 census proved to be a surprise. Predictions from the 1990 census projected the US population in 2000 to be 275 million but it turned out to be 281 million, higher than even the 'high series' projection of 1990. Of particular significance, immigration was higher than expected and the birth-rate of native-born Americans also exceeded forecasts. Immigration between 1990 and 2000 was recorded at over 11 million, as against the six million in the 1970s and 7 million in the 1980s. Actual 2000 figures could be higher since an estimated 8 to 9 million illegal immigrants entered the country in the 1990s and not all may have been counted in the census. This immigration increase is expected to have a compounding effect in future years as the fertility rate of non-Hispanic whites was slightly over 1.8 and blacks was 2.1, whereas the Hispanic fertility rate was nearly 3.0. Accordingly, the US total population rate is expected to continue to grow.

Europe has also experienced an immigration increase and, in fact, took in slightly more immigrants than the USA in the period 1985–95. Since 1995, European immigration rate has decreased, possibly because of increasing barriers to immigration. Overall, since 1950, Europe has received fewer immigrants than the USA. *The Economist* (August 24, 2002) advises that most demographers predict that over the next few decades immigration into Europe will be much lower than into the USA. Some project the immigration breakdown for Europe and the USA between 2000 and 2050 to be in the region of 28 per cent to Europe and 72 per cent to the USA.

This difference in immigration rates and fertility rates between Europe and the USA shows up dramatically in the expectations of age distribution. Bill Frey, a demographer at the University of Michigan, calculates the median age in 2003 to be 35.5 years in the USA and 37.7 years in Europe. Applying current trend, Frey forecasts that the mean age of population in the year 2050 will be 36.2 in America and 52.7 in Europe. The forecasted difference in the age profile of Europe and the USA has major policy implications that are pertinent to care-givers and care providers. The 'dependency ratio' – the number of children and elders for each working-age person – starts to move in opposite directions for the two regions. For benchmark purposes, in 2000 the percentage of the population under the age of 15 was 19 per cent in the UK (slightly higher than the EU average) and 21 per cent in the USA. At the other end of the spectrum, the percentage of the population over the age of 65 was 16 per cent in the UK and 13 per cent in the USA (Hale, 2000).

As well as influencing birth-rates and dependency rates, the influx of migrant labour (and associated work, performance, and training and development issues for both the existing and mobile staff) necessitates a response from organisations and HRD professionals. What this response might be is covered in more depth in the following chapters, but the inter-relations of the issue are worth noting here.

Technological advances and human capital

Technological advances impact upon the area in several key ways that are linked to the ability to handle complex information more easily and at a distance, and to the need to retain and retrain those with the ability to manage the technological systems. Organisations are now able to manage their internal statistics and systems more fluidly, such that keeping track of flexible working and a wide system of varied benefits no longer presents the logistical problem that it used to. Organisations are now able to offer tailored packages to meet the needs of individuals if they so wish.

Similarly, because of advances in technology, organisations are now able to offer many of their employees the opportunity to work from home, for at least part of the time. In this way the home computer becomes the equivalent to a workplace terminal and the interface between the two becomes transparent. It becomes a flexible package that lends itself to use by non-care-givers as well as care-givers. This also means that 'home' can be a mobile concept, and parts of the 'organisation' can be located across the world – as, for example, the rise of call centres in Bangalore that operate transparently, such that a person making a local call to a company in the UK does not realise that the call is actually being answered and managed by someone in India. This fundamentally changes the traditional notions of work and organisation. Wherever they are located, skilled individuals can work for several organisations from across the world at the same time and, similarly, wherever they are located, adept organisations can call upon the services of skilled individuals from across the world.

Skilled workers need no longer be bound by geography or loyalty – they can sell their human capital to those that offer the best packages of pay and benefits. Human capital can be seen as the knowledge that individuals acquire during their life and use to produce goods, services or ideas in market or non-market circumstances. Organisations, however, have been slow to realise the value of human capital, and slow to develop the skills to be able to evaluate it (Brown, 2002). Human capital can be seen as an intangible asset of the organisation, and is one that can be poached by other organisations and needs support and development to flourish.

Valuable knowledge and skills get lost or diluted as disenfranchised employees move on, therefore one of the key challenges to organisations is to retain their human capital. Organisations also need to keep updating the skills of their employees. In an effort to enhance loyalty, some organisations are also retraining employees who are taking career breaks, in the hope that they will return – with their updated knowledge.

These points parallel Drucker, who suggests that management still assumes the interchangeability of manual workers (even while acknowledging turnover, rehiring and retraining costs, manual workers are still seen as a cost). He argues that much of this goes back to the fact that the means of production were not owned by the worker, and in spite of possession of valuable experience, the only place where that experience could be used was in the workplace. The means of production were not portable. 'But knowledge workers own the means of production. It is between their ears' (Drucker, 1999: 149). Owning the means of production gives knowledge-workers mobility.

Considerations for the future

Demographic projections paint a stark picture of increasing mobility, and of shifts in the pattern and age of the workforce. The nature and location of work is changing. Similarly, projections show that the nature and structure of family life is also changing. In the following chapters we look at the implications these hold for each of the main stakeholders – individuals, organisations and the State – but before doing so we devote the remainder of this chapter to exploring the core of what *might* be prescribed for the future.

Under the present structure, employees with care-giving responsibilities are under intense time (and energy) pressure when attempting simultaneously to achieve their full individual potential and to care for their dependants. For many, the result can be to disadvantage all parties – employer, dependants and self. As employers began to perceive that the pressures being endured by their care-giver employees were negatively affecting the firms' operations, in their own interests they began installing family-friendly policies. Some of those employers have found that the unencumbered non-care-giver may also have commitments outside of their employment and feel that concessions to ease the plight of their care-giving colleagues have been given at their expense. For example, Lizotte (2001) suggests that most companies seem to favour strongly family-oriented benefit packages, letting their single workers all but languish in the shadows.

Cliff Baizer (2001), adjunct professor at Bently College, admonishes 'It becomes a question of what does "work life balance" mean to people who don't have kids?' He cites that on-site day care and family health plans are top on the list of most parents with young children, but reminds that they do little to entice prospective employees who have no dependants. Baizer emphasises that employers have to expand their model of work–family thinking. Many other scholars and practitioners have advocated that management expand its thinking to recognise the fundamental reality that work is part and parcel of life and does not exist outside of life.

These thoughts resonate with the explosion of alternative forms of working, such as the portfolio worker, the home worker, a mobile workforce, small enterprises and technology firms. Each of these breaks away from the traditional form of 9–5 full-time employment, and each necessitates a more flexible approach to labour management, training and development.

Flexibility is the key

Shore (1998) maintains that scholars agree that individuals can better manage long work hours with the unpredictable demands of dependant care when given a measure of control over where and when work is to be done. It is widely recognised that work–life balance is about improved health and productivity, and about keeping employees engaged with the organisation, including recognising their lives and commitments outside of work. The Industrial Society (IS) found that the long-hours issue and the growing levels of absence demonstrate the imbalance in work–life, yet IS research also found a gap between the demand and the take up by employees of work–life options.

Moen and Yu (2000) found that the factors associated with quality of life are similar across gender, with conditions at work serving as key predictors of life quality for both men and women. Specifically, having a demanding job and job insecurity are associated with a low quality of life, while having a supportive supervisor is positively linked to quality of life outcomes. Work hours and work-hour preferences matter as well. Men and women in couples where both spouses work regular (39–45) full-time hours tend to score highly on indicators of life quality, while those working long hours and those preferring to work less are less likely to achieve such a high score.

Richard Reeves, Director of Future, Industrial Society (UK), cautions that the real divide in the workplace is not between those who work long hours and those who work short hours but between those who are in control of their hours, the time sovereigns, and those whose hours are controlled for them, the time subjects. Reeves maintains that work–life balance has successfully raised awareness about work time but that the number of hours worked is only half the story. He sums up thus: 'The more say the workers have over their working time, the more sovereign they are, the less stress they feel and the more able they are to balance home and work.' Judith Doyle, co-author of IS's *Time Out*, reports:

> Time sovereignty recognises that for many workers the divide between work and life is not always clear-cut. Modern lives are less easy to be cut up into chunks of 'work' here and 'life' there. Employers need to start judging by task rather than time. Control over workers' time decreases workers' motivation and increases the risks to profitability and productivity. Ultimately, the time sovereigns are more likely to be the star performers when it comes to bottom-line contribution.
>
> (Doyle, 2001)

Lizotte (2001) reports that flexible scheduling is among the most appreciated benefits because employers don't 'own' their employees' time. Therefore, employees appreciate it whenever they can obtain control over their own time. Barney Olmsted, co-director of the scheme New Ways to Work in San Francisco, says that managers need to give all employees as much control as possible over their lives. He counsels firms to think work/life instead of work/family, which he claims will 'be rewarded with the enthusiasm of a workforce bent on excellence'.

Worklife Report 2001 reveals that recent data show that fewer then one in two workers have control over their hours. Yet 54 per cent of those who decide their own working hours are completely or very satisfied with their job compared to 42 per cent of those whose hours are decided by their employer. Among the younger workers the numbers are even higher. Eighty per cent of those born after 1963 – Generation 'Xers' – feel they would be more likely to stay in their jobs if their employer allowed for a balance and this rises to 93 per cent among those aged 18–25. The report comments that in most organisations there will be some staff who are less able to be time sovereign than others: front-line service staff, administrative personnel, production-line workers, for example. Granting more sovereignty to one group of workers can therefore create tensions, which have to be managed carefully.

The following three chapters take a look at some of the tensions being experienced by the three parties involved – the employees, the companies and the State.

11 Tensions for the individuals (and their families)

In this chapter the tensions being experienced by employees with care-giving priorities are explored in the light of the competing elements of time and resources. The chapter starts with a brief overview of the discussions earlier in the book that emphasise the impact that caring for dependants has upon individuals and their careers, before addressing the tensions and strategies for managing them.

Working women face work/life conflicts resulting from their continuing role as primary care-givers for their children and elders and their care-taker role in the home. Men who hold the key caring role for dependants are in a similar position. Husbands in dual-career households (67 per cent) face new workplace stresses as they have assumed greater responsibility at home. Forty-six per cent of workers are parents of children under the age of 18 (with 20 per cent of these being single parents). Older workers are often unwilling or physically unable to meet full-time work schedules. More and more workers are facing ever-greater family demands on their time. Time spent on the job (total working hours) has increased since the 1980s and some see their jobs as becoming more demanding and less secure than in the past. As the population ages these demands are likely to increase. It has been evident over the past several years that a 'time bind' has been created by the simultaneous rise in family and workplace pressures – and it appears to be getting worse (Saltzstein, Ting and Saltzstein, 2001).

The qualitative themes that emerged from the written-survey respondents centred around the perception that long hours are required in order to be considered for training and promotion; the perception that part-time employees are unlikely to be considered for promotion; the desire to put family responsibilities first; and the concern over work/life issues. Each of these themes reflects the tensions over time, resources, and the desire for changed priorities.

Freedom to pursue a career

Part II showed that relative freedom to pursue a career becomes *the* defining factor of the care-giving/career-progression debate. How well home-base is covered establishes the parameters within which the alternatives for utilising time and resources are examined and priorities are established. The question 'Is home-base covered?' encapsulates a host of other supporting questions – variations on the themes of time, resource, and the setting of priorities – all requiring the attention of the family-unit decision maker(s).

Not all employees wish to aggressively pursue careers. Some choose not to pursue careers but may not have much choice about the need to generate income. Some choose to have a career but find themselves unexpectedly caring for dependants. However, as Moen and Yu (2000) say, jobs and career paths are constructed in ways that presume workers are without family. 'We hold that work hours represent, perhaps, the most fundamental aspect of structural lag.' They maintain that there are few realistic options for working less than full time without jeopardising benefits and future advancement. Similarly, Woodall and Winstanley (1998) cite a number of researchers that maintain that management is stereotyped as a male role and that the stereotyping is based upon the foundations of a continuous, unbroken organisational career in which work is the primary source of identity for males.

Care-givers and part-time work

Many care-givers attempt to meet their responsibilities by moving to part-time work and so better balance their care-giving with the needs of income generation and career development. For example, Felmlee (1984) found that women were likely to move from full- to part-time work because of young children, and Rosin and Korabik (1990) stated that some women may choose to leave the workforce because of heavy demands of preschool children. Similarly, one US government study of family care-givers found that 23 per cent of working women had to reduce working hours, 35 per cent rearranged their schedules and 25 per cent took time off without pay to care for elderly parents (Hordern, 1996). Some articles (Hordern, 1996; Rodgers and Rodgers, 1989) have suggested that some 33 per cent of all working families are (or soon will be) involved with elder-care. The respondents discussed in Part II indicated elder-care responsibilities in only 6 per cent of the cases (same percentage for both UK and USA). The low percentage of respondents involved with elder-care could help explain why elder-care has not yet reached the corporate 'radar' screen of the organisations that participated in the research, and could be a function of that sector.

There are disadvantages to moving to part-time work, however. Reich (2000) commented that the press of paid work tends to increase the regimentation of everything else – the nature of the work can become less satisfying and the complications of handover to another (particularly in job-share arrangements) can create additional demands. In addition, the evidence presented in Part II shows that part-time workers receive less training than full-time workers and are less likely to be considered for promotion. Three comments from respondents had exceptional explanatory power: 'part-timers are here to support the full-timers'; another commented that her boss asked her why he should promote her when he could promote someone who was at work full time; 'working part time – unable to be fully involved in issues' was the third. Within the traditional masculine culture of the workplace, there remains the belief that full-time workers seek a career, whilst part-time workers only seek a job for 'pin money'.

Most of the literature seeking to explain the predicament of the part-timer does so in economic terms. Ragins and Sundstrom (1989) asserted that increased career interruptions and role overload from home demands may result in an unfavourable perception by the decision makers who fast-track potential managerial candidates. This leads to a double-bind situation in which care-givers are at a disadvantage both because they work part time and because they receive less development. One empirical finding from Part II that stood out from this was that several executive interview participants worked part time (all females), one was in a job-share arrangement. One can speculate that the issue did not impact upon them in as dramatic a manner as upon lower-grade employees: they were in a position to be able to pay for care-giving more easily than were lower-paid workers and, as they were at the height of their careers, they were possibly not so dependent upon receiving in-house development. However, during an executive interview one female executive revealed that although career aspirations were still evident in both her own and her job-share partner's mind, she did not feel that either of them would be seriously considered for promotion until they returned to full-time employment. Essentially, she felt that even though performing outstandingly in a part-time executive job-sharing position, their careers were still 'on hold'.

The need for long hours

> **Sandra** is 33 years old, has a high school/secondary school education and works as a Customer Service Clerk. She is married, her husband works full time and they have an infant child. Sandra works part time, 25 hours per week, with travelling to and from work requiring an additional 3 hours per week. She estimates that she earns 25 per cent of the household income. Sandra is able to accept assignments outside of normal hours only sometimes, whether she has notice or not. She has this to say: 'At the moment, with my family commitments, I feel I cannot take on any more responsibility. I don't have the time for taking the training, and working the extra hours required for earning promotion is just not possible for me at this stage of our lives.'

Both the literature and the empirical work discussed in this book show that one of the key drivers to the discrimination against care-givers is that they cannot always work the long hours and at the times required by the organisation, and are thus seen to lack commitment. As shown in the previous part, long hours are seen as being an essential factor in determining fitness for promotion or receipt of training leading to promotion.

The long-hours culture has a particular impact upon those with dependants, who often find themselves at a serious disadvantage in the workplace. Non-care-givers were found to work longer hours than care-givers and were more available to work extra-hour assignments than care-givers. Non-care-givers also received more management-training opportunities and participated in formal career-development plans to a greater extent than care-givers. The litany of comments from the survey respondents was long – and uniform – and revealed the pervasive perception was that long hours were required to gain the recognition necessary for promotion or for receipt of training leading to promotion.

Factors in the care-giving equation

For those care-giver employees who do wish to pursue careers, the interlocking relationship between working long hours for promotion, having family commitments and working part time exposes the setting of acceptable priorities in the question: 'is home-base covered?'. Does the employee care-giver have someone at home – either part time or full time (that is, not gainfully employed) – that can shoulder the major portion of the time burden for the family unit so as to free the employee to pursue the resources portion of the family-unit burden? If this is the case, then the tension is relieved and family priorities have been expanded (time available to do both care-giving and resource earning). In many – if not most – cases, home-base is not so conveniently covered. (The US Bureau of Labor states that only 16 per cent of full-time workers go home to a non-working spouse. The percentage of US homes with part-time working spouses was not available to this study. (Schwartz 1992.))

Lone parents are at the sharp end of balancing life/work tensions. They need to look to their own resources or what the organisation or State can provide, and are particularly vulnerable to the poverty trap mentioned above. In dual-earner families, several different strategies for coping with work/family demands have been observed by Becker and Moen (1999). They point out that as jobs and circumstances change within families, so too do the expectations and forms of adaptation. Becker and Moen (1999) highlight the three basic strategies observed in families attempting to manage as best they can within the existing parameters of the lag in culture and organisation of work and careers. They emphasise that the strategies typically remain a variant of the breadwinner/homemaker model, replacing it with what might be called a neo-traditional career/job model. The three strategies observed were all variations of 'scaling back', that is, the process by which dual-earners attempt to circumscribe home and protect it from the encroachments of work. In essence the couples were attempting to confront the 'hierarchy of values that places the demands of work over those of family'. In the analysis of their 117 interview study, Becker and Moen found that the respondents (male and female; two-thirds with children, one-third without children) revealed three specific couple level strategies for scaling back. First was the reduction of work hours. One-third of the interviewed group placed limits on the number of hours they would work and reduced long-term expectations for career advancement in order to spend more time with the family. Of those utilising this strategy, one-third were men and two-thirds were women. The men were reported as almost always associating placing hour limits with their experiences of fathering and desire to spend more time with their children. For women, the placing of limits on hours of work was typically associated with having young children at home; however, unlike the men, a significant proportion of the women placed limits on work across all ages and life-course stages, even when there were no children at home. The second scaling-back strategy was differentiating between job and career. Within the group, jobs were understood to be *ad hoc* and flexible, more about making money than intrinsic satisfaction, whereas careers were felt to progress in a straight line, with change less often, and rewarding in themselves. In 40 per cent of the couples interviewed, it was perceived by both that one person had a job and the other a career. It was generally understood that the person with the career would take advantage of career opportunities when they arose and the other, with the job, would follow and accommodate. The woman had the job and the man the career in over two-thirds of the sample interviewed. The third strategy was trading off. Just over a third of the couples adopted a strategy of trading off either job/career (which could be revised over the life course) or who would place work-hour limits to spend more time at home (which, again, could be revised over the life course).

For those care-givers relying upon care providers outside of the home, the tension focuses on such questions as:

- Who is to be the care provider (non-resident family, extended family, neighbour, nursery, day care, after school, etc.)?
- When and for how long per day will the provider services be available (early, late, day only, anytime, etc.)?
- Where is the care providing to take place (at home, someone else's home, professional facility, near home, near work, convenient, out of the way)? Is late pick-up possible? Are there late-pick-up penalty charges?
- How much resources will be required (which begets the question 'who pays' – the individual, the organisation, the State?)?

- Does the care-giver make full use of existing routes of support?
- Can the job commitments be altered to allow more flexible working hours or more home working?

Each of these begets other questions: What are the issues surrounding the subcontracting of care-giving services? Why do some care-givers not make full use of existing systems of support? Whose responsibility is it to establish systems of support? How can alternative patterns of work be negotiated? Does the answer to these questions differ according to the care-giver's disposable income and organisational status?

To subcontract?

Robert Reich (2000), former US Secretary of Labor in the first Clinton Administration, reviewed the trend for working mothers in the USA: 15 per cent of women with children under the age of 6 were in paid work at mid century versus 65 per cent at the end of the twentieth century. He commented that all sorts of things that used to be done by families are now being subcontracted to specialists – house cleaning, child- and elder-care, food preparation, even dog-walking. 'The test a family uses to decide whether to subcontract a particular task is just like the test used by a company considering whether to "out-source" a particular function. Can the subcontractor do the task as well as the family member can do it, but more cheaply, considering the alternative uses of the family member's time?' (Reich, 2000).

He notes that as both men and women work harder for pay, they're subcontracting out more of what were once family responsibilities:

> By far the biggest family subcontract is child care. Today most children under the age of five – more than 10 million of them – need to be looked after while their mothers and fathers go to work. Forty-four percent of these children are cared for by relatives, including older siblings; 30 percent, by staff of day-care centres or nursery schools; 15 percent, by other adults in private homes; and the rest, by nannies, neighbours, or baby sitters. A significant portion of these children don't get much personal attention in this hodgepodge of child-care arrangements. ... The amount and quality of personal attention varies directly with its price.
>
> (Reich, 2000)

The UK provides significantly more state support for care-givers than is available in the USA; however, it is worth noting that some UK individuals (especially younger employees) can find themselves in what has been coined as a 'poverty trap'. Non-working care-givers receive support, as do working care-givers, but those that are working have to contribute towards their care facilities. The means-tested benefits are reduced to the point where some actually end up with more money by not working. Consequently, they are caught in a 'poverty trap' that keeps those with dependants from returning to work.

Another factor that can prevent care-givers from returning to work is the perception that subcontracted care-giving might be less beneficial than home care – if not actually harmful. Galinsky, Bond and Friedman (1993) suggest that most employees perceive home and family-based care to be less potentially harmful to their children than other arrangements. Although no scientifically supported data is known to have been generally accepted to date, Galinsky *et al.* detected that a perception exists that day care poses a risk to healthy child development and that many employed parents, especially mothers, experience significant guilt feelings that they are harming their children. Morgan (1996), of the Institute of Economic Affairs, reports that research suggests that when compared with children cared for at home, children in child-care may be disadvantaged in educational performance, behaviour and attachment to their mothers.

Fitzgerald (2001) reports a federal (US) study, released in April 2001, wherein researchers reported that regardless of where the child was cared for (day-care centre, someone's home or with a relative), children who spent more time in non-maternal care were more likely to have behaviour problems than children who spent less time in child-care. It was noted that children who spend long hours in child-care are more likely to be aggressive (bully, fight, be mean to peers) and disobedient when they reach kindergarten age. Tracking 1,300 infant, toddler and preschool-years children nationwide, the study did not identify any specific number of hours in non-maternal care before the child became problematic but indicated that it was a gradually increasing effect. Jay Belsky, one of the principal investigators, formerly a Pennsylvania State University researcher and more recently of the University of London's Birkbeck College, stated that the connection between long hours in child-care and behaviour problems held true even when the quality of care was high and mothers were attentive at home. The researchers noted that the patterns held for both girls and boys and for children from families both poor and well-off. The report cautioned that the behaviour of the studied children was still within the 'normal' range on a standardised rating system – at the high end of normal but not enough to diagnose them with a behaviour disorder. The researchers also reported that children who spent their early years in high-quality child-care – particularly good day-care centres – were more likely to score high on measures such as language, cognitive ability and memory skills at the age of $4\frac{1}{2}$.

These figures can be set alongside those of the Manhattan-based Public Agenda group, which found that 70 per cent of parents of children aged 5 or younger believe it best for one parent to be at home with them;

60 per cent doubt that even a top-notch day-care centre is a close equivalent of a stay-at-home parent; 63 per cent worry about physical or sexual abuse in day-care centres; and 78 per cent say the best alternative to parent care is to rely on grandparents or other close relatives (Rasberry, 2000). Perhaps Schwartz (1992) spoke for many when she wrote: 'Since high quality affordable day care was rare, many worried parents were permanently anxious about their children.'

This raises the question of who sets the standards for the subcontracted care-giving. Individuals do not often have the ability to perform accurate benchmarking and evaluation of the facilities. This is, however, one aspect of support that both the organisations and the State can provide, and is addressed in the following chapters.

Looking to the organisation

Employees are increasingly looking to the organisation to help them meet their needs. They seek more flexible patterns of work and acceptance of their care-giving role. The survey respondents reported in Part II emphasised that given a choice between work and care-giving, the responsibilities of the latter had to come first. Many comments were essentially reflections or frustrations with the constraints imposed by their chosen priority – care-giving. Other comments were more in the nature of 'complaints' or 'solutions' offered concerning the wisdom of long hours being equated with 'commitment' and commitment being seen to come only from full-time employees. The following chapter looks more closely at organisational strategies in support of care-givers, but it is interesting to note that both in the literature and in the empirical evidence presented in Part II there is a mismatch between organisations offering support and employees making use of it. Indeed, research conducted by Taylor Nelson Softres (2002) shows that whilst 50 per cent of their organisations (from a sample of 1,000 replies from training and development personnel) offered care-givers the opportunity to work from home, only 14 per cent of the respondents made use of this facility.

As reported in Part II, many of the respondents felt reluctant to invoke their organisations' support, giving reasons such as thereby signalling that they were less interested in their career, or the lack of sympathy or support shown by their supervisor. We might also speculate that given the difference between the US and UK cultures in their willingness to be open about financial issues and the need for support (as discussed in Chapter 4), some respondents might be reluctant to seek organisational support because to do so might be perceived by colleagues to indicate that the care-giver is losing the struggle to balance home and work commitments. There was also an indication that some employees felt that if they took reduced work hours their colleagues would have to shoulder an additional burden of work. The resolution of these issues necessitates a shift in the attitudes and behaviours in the workplace. This is not to say, however, that the individual cannot have an effect. Several of the respondents discussed in Part 2 explained how they had sought more organisational support – and achieved it. To create the climate for a needed shift in attitudes and behaviours, individuals – both care-givers and non-care-givers – must make their views known.

Not all employees seek the same sort of support. It might be that the organisation does offer support for care-givers, but not the right sort for particular individual needs. For example, as discussed in the previous part, there was a plea from some in the lower levels of the organisations for employer-provided crèche facilities. In contrast, care-giving executives were less keen – they had other arrangements in place. By stating their needs and asserting their value to the organisation, individuals might be able to help the organisation develop a flexible raft of supportive policies.

By asserting their value to the organisation it might be that one day care-givers will be assessed by the work they actually do rather than judged as not being committed to the organisation because they do not put in the long hours that those with fewer outside priorities can manage. They might then receive more development opportunities and training, and thus be seen to be more suitable for promotion.

The value of the individual

Without such development the career options of care-givers are limited and the outside priorities of others are ignored. Development and training can impose further burdens on the care-giver, such that they choose not to enhance their career in this way. Similarly, organisations can be justifiably reluctant to expend money on individuals who could be perceived as less loyal, both because of their apparent lack of commitment due to an inability to work long hours, and because their care-giving responsibility makes them more likely to leave. However, it might benefit the organisation to take the longer view in this instance. For example, Skapinker (2002) reports that McKinsey offers an extensive training package and yet plans on losing about 80 per cent of the people it hires in 5 years or less to competitor organisations. It wishes these people well and they part on good terms. In doing so it maintains a network of McKinsey alumni that help out each other and McKinsey in the future. This sort of approach requires a change of attitudes and behaviour on behalf of most organisations.

In talking of the value of the individual we are referring back to the discussion on human capital in the previous chapter. Care-givers can hold a wealth of knowledge that, because of their circumstances, is unused and often unrecognised. 'Knowledge management' is now a regularly used term, and a survey by KPMG (CIPD, 1999) found that 43 per cent of the hundred leading British companies in 1998 had a specific knowledge-management programme (one designed to use 'the ideas and experiences of employees, customers and suppliers to improve the organisation's performance' (Human Resources Institute, 2002)). All employees, whether part time, full time, care-givers or non-care-givers, are valuable resources, and keeping the information they represent available to the organisation may give that organisation a competitive advantage over others. It is held that for this to happen the organisation will need to inspire loyalty, and to ensure that the information is on hand and up to date. Many feel that it is in the organisation's best interest to provide benefits that enhance the care-giver's loyalty, allow flexible working that maintains the care-giver's availability, and develop, train and retrain him or her (regardless of whether that person is on a career break or not) so that the care-giver can contribute to his or her fullest potential when with the organisation. These are discussed in the next chapter but are raised here because they are unlikely to occur without being championed by the care-giving employees. Individuals do have the ability to put pressure on the organisations to change, and many can vote with their feet if change is not forthcoming.

Voting with the feet

The increasing mobility of employees and the increasingly geographically free nature of the work required were discussed in the previous chapter. Both of these have an impact upon the care-giver. As was shown in the empirical evidence, the need to move with the job can cause havoc to carefully laid care-giving plans, and can lead to the refusal of promotions and so on. However, the development of technology and associated working practices means that many jobs no longer have to be associated with a particular location. Skilled care-givers are in an ideal position to work from home whilst meeting the needs of one or more employers. As the population declines and the nature of work continues to adjust to technological advances we anticipate that the wealth of human capital embedded in care-givers will give them the power of the market – those that have skills that are wanted by organisations will be able to negotiate the packages that best suit them and their responsibilities.

Of course, not all care-givers have such skills. Indeed, the evidence presented in Part II shows that employees who are care-givers and who have full-time working partners are less well educated than those without care-giving responsibilities or those who have care-giving responsibilities but have someone at home full time or part time who shoulders the major portion of the care-giving responsibility. Clearly, an issue for the less well educated is whether or not they deem it in their balanced best interest to pursue further education and, if so, where and how such can be accomplished.

Seeking the enhanced package

Individual recourse to public discourse as an option for changing the present state of affairs is unlikely to be overlooked. It might be that as mobility increases individuals turn to those employers who offer not just enhanced pay but also the best 'whole person' package, including recognition of the need of many employees – care-givers and not a few of the unencumbered who also hold passionate 'outside' priorities – for *flexible* working environments and the needs of individuals for support in their self-development, including training and career development. We have emphasised 'flexible' here because it is clear from the empirical data that 'different folks require different strokes'. Those with greater disposable income and organisational status face a different set of challenges to those without. For example, higher-paid earners might be able to afford good-quality private care whilst having greater organisational responsibility – and thus have greater flexibility to work long hours without notice and greater ability to respond to a need for mobility. They do not need a crèche that ties them to regular hours and one location. In contrast, a low-paid worker without the resources to evaluate the best care facilities for their young child or to cover the time and costs of transporting that child to be cared for might see a company crèche as a life-saver.

A flexible package that lends itself to use by non-care-givers as well as care-givers can also be seen as one way to minimise any backlash arising against what is perceived to be preferential treatment given to care-givers. As Young (1999) points out, one consequence of the majority of employees not having child-care responsibilities is a work/family backlash, which she describes as a controversy over the fundamental issue of what is fair. Although Dillner (2000) concluded that there was little substance in the allegations that raging resentment exists and the evidence presented in Part II partially supports Dillner's optimistic conclusion, negative comments were received evidencing a small but persistent backlash. Literature alleging a backlash is growing in volume. Further research on perceptions of undue favouritism to care-givers is needed, on a timely basis, to assist those charged with policy formulation in this work–life area. We suggest that a flexible package that lends itself to use by non-care-givers as well as care-givers will be an essential component of any resolution.

Summing up

The key tensions for the individual care-giver lie in balancing time and resources. These lead to the need to set priorities, in which the care-giving role takes precedence. Employees are looking to their employer and/or to the State for relief from the 'time bind' created by the simultaneous rise in family and workplace pressures. Many, unencumbered by care-giving responsibilities, also have 'outside' activities to which they attach a high priority. They too seek relief from the 'time bind'. This is compounded by the organisational culture in which long hours are seen to equal commit-ment, and in which care-givers receive less training and development and fewer promotional opportunities. Strategies for addressing these issues have been discussed, and whilst some of these can be addressed by the individual, many require the organisation, in their own self-interest, to adopt a less traditional approach.

We suggest, however, that the shift in the nature of work and the emerging population demographics enhance the individual's ability to vote with the feet, and thus to apply pressure upon the organisation. The following chapter reviews some of the challenges facing the organisation and outlines possible strategies to meet these.

12 Tensions for the companies

This chapter explores the challenges for organisations in managing care-givers and in fostering organisational health in a world in which the (care-giving) workforce is ageing and mobile. The chapter starts with a brief overview of the discussions earlier in the book that emphasise the problems that face organisations who do not adapt to the needs of their care-giving workforce, before addressing the tensions and strategies for managing them.

The first part of the book discussed the traditional form that many organisations still adhere to – that in which the male is assumed to be the breadwinner and the female is assumed to stay at home and look after care-giving. The empirical evidence discussed in the second part shows that despite changes in society these traditional structures and assumptions are still alive and well. Chapter 10, at the beginning of this part, challenges those assumptions. We suggest that the declining birth-rate in combination with technological advances will have a major effect upon organisations. As the population ages, a greater number of the working population are likely to become care-givers, and also likely to become more mobile. At present care-givers are perceived to be lacking commitment to the organisation, are given less training and development and are passed over for promotion, and, as such, they represent a wasted resource. Similar 'lack of commitment' perceptions and consequences are likely to be experienced by those unencumbered by care-giving responsibilities but who hold high non-company-connected 'outside' priorities. As skilled labour becomes scarcer, and the knowledge skilled workers hold becomes more valuable, Drucker's (1999) advice to treat workers as assets rather than costs will become increasingly pertinent. Neither we, nor any of the respondents discussed in Part II, are suggesting that organisations are deliberately disadvantaging care-givers. What we are talking about here, however, is more than just introducing policies. We are talking about a radical change in attitudes and behaviour, and are suggesting that this is necessary for organisational survival.

Noel, Senior Vice President of Corporate IT, is 38 years old, married, has two children and his partner works full time. The children attend primary school and an after-school programme. He drops the children off at school in the mornings and his wife picks them up at 6 o'clock in the evening. Noel said: 'A lot of people start working quite young and throw themselves into their work and would be there all night – and weekends too, if required. Then everybody grows up, has families, can't work the hours they used to, and that leaves us dependent on things like overtime and goodwill. One thing that helps persuade me that we must change is that I feel the same way about my family, too. We have to deal with it in whatever ways will work – whether it's time off or whatever it is. There is so much demand for IT people that some prefer to work just 4 days, be well paid, and off 3 days. We have to look at ways of balancing between getting the right amount of resources on projects within the company so we can deliver what we need, but we also must keep Bill and Betty happy within the family. We have a lot of part-time working in IT at the moment and it was a deliberate thing. We did an advert asking if anyone wanted to come back into work for a limited amount of time and we got some good deals through that. It might be more management and a little more pain when you try to develop projects or people, but we shouldn't shy away from new approaches to get good people.'

The current situation from the organisational perspective

Much of this book so far has concentrated upon the impact that care-giving has upon the individual's career progression (as one might expect from the title) but it is worth noting that organisations are also adversely affected by care-giving. Human Resources Institute (2000) conducted a survey of 150 US-based global corporations in order to examine the extent to which care-giving duties were affecting their workforce. Nearly 60 per cent of respondents said that productivity was lost to a high or moderate degree as a result of work-day interruptions caused by care-giving (including making personal phone calls, leaving suddenly because of a care-giving crisis and leaving work early or arriving late). Fifty-six per cent reported high or moderate loss of productivity caused by care-giving-related absenteeism, 54 per cent reported disruption related to rearranging schedules because of care-giving and 44 per cent reported time lost because of people thinking about care-giving problems. The report sets the cost of care-giving to the USA at US$196 billion (of which US$11 billion to US$29 billion is for elder-care) but excludes secondary costs, such as the cost of health problems of the carers – including stress, exhaustion and frustration – with 60 per cent of people caring for elderly parents requiring treatment for depression.

A picture of support

Despite the lack of support for care-givers evidenced in the data discussed in Part II, many organisations report that they already have care-giving policies in place. A UK survey of 2,000 management professionals reported in the *Leadership and Organization Development Journal* (2000) found that employers were offering a wide range of perks to recruit and train staff ranging from family-friendly policies to pet insurance. It noted that in anticipation of legislation, 57 per cent of respondents reported their organisations offering parental/domestic leave, 75 per cent reported them offering part-time working as an option, job sharing was available in 57 per cent of the organisations and one-third offered teleworking. Also mentioned were newer-trend perks to help employees with balancing work and life – 39 per cent offered stress helplines, 25 per cent offered financial planning, 12 per cent offered dry-cleaning facilities, 10 per cent offered personal car insurance, 8 per cent offered food-shopping facilities, 3 per cent offered pet insurance and 2 per cent offered film/video-rental facilities. Significantly, 40 per cent of those surveyed offered career breaks and 24 per cent offered sabbaticals. The report noted, however, that child-care remained an area where few employers offer on-site options, with only one in ten surveyed having a workplace nursery and 2 per cent offering provision for after-school care.

A picture of participation?

Interestingly, although the respondents were able to give details of their organisational policies, the HRI (2000) report found that 80 per cent either did not know or had to guess at the number of care-givers in their workforce. There was also variation in how much the organisation was willing to spend on assistance to care givers: 20 per cent said they would spend US$21 or higher per employee per year, with 54 per cent spending US$10 or less; 33 per cent said employees should share the cost of the services, with only 4 per cent saying they should not and the remainder saying that it depended upon the service.

McCurry (2002) holds that the term 'family friendly' has been replaced by 'work/life balance' in the UK in recognition that all staff, not just working parents, need to be included in the arrangements. He reports the establishment of Employers for Work/Life Balance, an alliance of twenty-two leaders, supported by the Prime Minister, who believe that the introduction of work/life policies has benefited their organisations. The group, chaired by Peter Ellwood, Group Chief Executive of Lloyds TSB, aims to share best practice and establish a one-stop shop for employers on work/life issues. Many in the USA also recognise that the term 'family friendly' has served its purpose of bringing national attention to the conflict between working and living and that it's time to move on. They appreciate that bringing the plight of the employee with family responsibilities into the midst of the conflict has accelerated the attention given to the associated problems but feel that the term 'work–life' better represents the true issue, that is, it's not a choice between work or life; it's recognition of the reality that work is a part of life.

Not all employees might wish to make use of flexible working, and it is likely, as discussed earlier, that different groups of people will seek different packages. The availability of flexible-working practices to all, and not just to care-givers, is important because, as noted by Fuchs (1989), studies have shown that family-friendly programmes are 'amazingly' effective at reducing turnover but the potential of non-care-giver 'backlash' cannot be ignored. Ignoring the majority – even an almost silent one – cannot be a recipe for long-term success. Nor does it have to be an either/or game. Many have recorded their view that job satisfaction is about more than 'pay'. Training opportunities are often cited as having the potential for increasing employee satisfaction. Comments from the empirical data in Part II show respondents' desire for training, which they see as the key to the door for promotion. Organisations are both seeking talent and straining for ways to retain the best talent. Kristen Bowl, Manager of Media Affairs for the Society of Human Resource Management (HRM), points out that successful employers are finding new ways to be responsive, including the growing approach of offering benefits on a 'cafeteria plan'. Under this concept, companies place a dollar value on each individual benefit, and employees receive a lump sum with which to shop the menu. A worker who needs child-care, for example, is free to purchase that option, while her single co-worker may instead spend her benefit dollars on time in the gym. Both, however, are likely to opt for flextime. The tension for companies is not only to be fair to employees but to be seen as being fair to all of its employees

In the USA, the Institute of Management and Administration reports a survey of work/life programme managers by the Alliance of Work/Life Professionals (2002). The survey revealed that Employee Assistance Programs (EAP) and flexible schedules lead the list of work/life programmes. It reports that on average 56 per cent of employees took advantage of work/life programmes in 2001, an increase from 47 per cent in 1999. Percentage participation increases over 1999 were noted in the categories of EAP services, flexible schedules and child-care subsidies and a decrease from 1999 noted in organisations offering work/family seminars, child-care referrals, paid paternity leave, telecommuting and back-up child-care. The work/life professionals reported that financial resources devoted to work/life efforts were increased in 45 per cent of the reporting organisations, remained the same in 34 per cent of the organisations and decreased in 8 per cent. Since the report includes only firms employing work/life programme managers, the percentage of participation is unlikely to be representative of all firms yet the range and trends may broadly reflect present US practice.

The operational cost of care-giving initiatives

Perhaps Hobson, Delunas and Kesic (2001) laid out the challenge for the employer organisations by detailing the negative impact of the chronic inability of employees to balance work and life responsibilities – higher rates of absenteeism and turnover, reduced productivity, decreased job satisfaction, lower levels of organisational commitment and loyalty, and rising health-care costs. The difficulty seems to be in determining the true costs being experienced and the true saving to be expected. It seems undeniable that the costs/benefits will not be the same for all companies; nor will all of the separate initiatives in the package of work–life benefits have similar costs/benefits. Some things will be easier to define. As an example, turnover statistics are likely to be available in even the smallest firms, plus national statistics – with a commendable breakdown by position, organisation size, industry and so on – are available to assist management. That turnover represents a cost for employers is generally agreed, but computing the cost of turnover for the individual firm can be a show-stopper. Cost of turnover within the same company is likely to vary with a myriad of factors – position, experience, skill, interrelationships, length of time to replace, effort required to replace, employment and orientation costs and on and on. Absentee costs may be somewhat easier to calculate, but what about reduced productivity, decreased job satisfaction, lower levels of commitment, increased health-care costs? We all know that there are costs attached to each of these items – costs that come in real pounds or dollars – but how can one get a creditable calculation?

Firms are increasing the availability of work–family benefits to their employees, in part because they anticipate an increase in productivity, yet little more than anecdotal evidence supports this expectation. Meyer, Mukerjee and Sestero (2001) report one study attempting to determine which work/life initiatives had positive impact, which ones did not, and whether the amount provided was over or under providing the maximisation of profit. The report concluded that not all programmes have the same, or even a positive, impact upon profits. For instance, working from home showed positive benefits while job sharing had a significant negative impact on profits (firms should expand one form of scheduling and cut back on the other). Programmes such as flextime, compressed work-weeks and part-time work showed no significant impact on firms' profits. Increasing adoption benefits raised the profit rate while subsidising more dependants in on-site child-care reduced profits, indicating that the costs of this benefit could not be justified in terms of potential productivity gains – at least as the authors measured them. More detailed information should be sought by each company on both the magnitude and direction of the impact each programme has on its profits. It is crucial for choosing not only which programmes to adopt but also the degree to which these should be made available.

Bourg and Segal (1999) maintain: 'Although supportive family policies are often touted as having substantial payoffs for employers in terms of higher productivity, lower absenteeism and turnover and higher commitment, empirical evidence in support of these claims is rather scarce.' Perhaps Alan Saltzstein, Yuan Ting and Grace Saltzstein (2001) stated it best:

> After more than a decade of family friendly program development and implementation, we still know surprisingly little about who uses these programs. ... The possibility that specific programs and practices might have disparate effects on various subpopulations of employees has only just begun to be explored.

Certainly the empirical data discussed in the previous part of this book indicates that care-givers at different levels of disposable income and organisational status are likely to seek different forms of support from the organisation.

A brief catalogue of key indicators of an unsatisfactory work/life balance are said to include ill-health, low morale, lack of commitment, poor-quality work, absenteeism and high staff turnover. Some employers report significant business benefits from implementing family-friendly policies. These benefits are found equally in small and medium-sized firms. The benefits include: higher productivity; increased flexibility, for example to cover for absence and holidays; higher employee motivation and commitment; improved recruitment and retention. However, it has also been reported that employers may incur additional costs in adopting family-friendly policies, including increased managerial workloads. Only 18 per cent of the companies offering one or more flexible work arrangements perceive the costs of their investments in these policies as outweighing the benefits, whilst 36 per cent perceive these programmes to be cost neutral and 46 per cent perceive a positive return on their investment (The Families and Work Institute's 1998 Business Work–Life Study). The operative word is 'perceive' – they don't *know*. Without creditable knowledge of the cost/benefit of work–life initiatives, the organisation does not know its own self-interest.

Although the costs are generally claimed to be outweighed by the gains, work–life advocates maintain that the biggest obstacle to implementing good practice is in many cases the difficulty of persuading individual line managers to accept more flexible working arrangements. Advocates maintain that it is the individual line managers who hold the key to the future – or at least part of it!

The future-proof organisation?

Human Resource Institute (HRI) conducted a survey in Spring 2000 to determine the extent to which care-giving responsibilities were affecting the workforce. One hundred and fifty firms participated in the survey, most of which were US-based global firms. Approximately 70 per cent of the respondents felt that care-giving-related staffing problems, such as absenteeism and turnover, had increased in the last 10 years. American Association of Retired Persons (AARP) reported that the number of care-givers had tripled in the last decade and the trend is expected to increase. About 92 per cent of the respondents to the HRI survey believed that care-giving-related staffing problems would increase over the next 10-year period. The report commented: 'Based on the greying of the US population, this increase seems likely, if not inevitable.'

Chapter 10 laid the base for the argument that if organisations are to become, or remain, successful then they need to adapt to the changing nature of work and of the workforce. Part of this change is linked to the decrease in population and the associated increase in care-giving that is anticipated by demographers. At the same time as the needs of care-givers come to the fore, technological advances make possible forms of work and association between employee and employer that would have been hard to sustain previously. The sort of flexibility of working relationship that we suggest for care-givers might also help organisations attract (and retain) skilled workers (whether care-givers or not) in what is predicted to be an increasingly competitive and mobile labour market.

Need to maintain and retain

Even in the circumstance of 'temporarily' downsizing for strategic reasons, each of the organisations discussed in Part II expressed concern about their future ability to recruit and retain suitable talent. Each UK bank expressed concern over the competitive employee 'package' that was being required to entice talent to remain or relocate to their local area. All of the US banks expressed major concern over their 'turnover' rates (employee quit-and-replace rates). All three US banks had multiple HR personnel assigned full time to the sole task of recruiting. Some of the higher turnover rates of US versus UK banks may be explained by the difference in promotional policies followed in the two countries. The UK appears to prefer more promotion from within, while the USA appears to prefer to focus recruiting efforts on the particular expertise required. UK bank employees tend to look for promotional opportunities from within the bank itself and US bank employees apparently tend to look more to their professional specialty for promotion opportunities within the banking industry itself. This difference in promotion-seeking philosophy may help explain the very significant difference in the service years of UK and US bank employees. The UK evidenced longer service with less prior service with another employer, and the USA registered the opposite. However, this difference may also be a result of the UK banking tradition of 'a job for life', a tradition that may well be disappearing – as evidenced by the executive interviews. And, as it does disappear, UK firms may need to review their recruiting procedures.

As Jay Jamrog, the Executive Director of Human Resource Institute, said

> Workers aren't necessarily loyal to their employers anymore. Instead, they are more likely to be loyal to their profession, the projects they are working on, and their immediate supervisors. These are the big three. The survey shows that increases in pay aren't as big a deal. Low pay's a dissatisfier, but high pay won't keep people around by itself. The best people don't stay for the money alone. They stay because they are engaged and challenged by work that makes them better at what they do. They also want good training opportunities to keep themselves up to speed so that they can survive in the marketplace if they have to. The good part is that, with maybe the exception of some high-tech workers, most employees who get training are less likely to leave, even if they're more marketable. They will stay if they have a good relationship with their immediate boss and there's open communication with that boss.
>
> (Jamrog, 2001)

The sorts of working practices necessitated by the need to support caregivers also help retention. The Institute of Management and Administration (2002) report noted that employers are still in the process of developing benchmarks for determining the effectiveness for the employer of work/life programmes. Using a variety of data such as surveys and anecdotal evidence, the Institute reported that employer work/life professionals estimated benefits of work/life programmes as follows: attracting/retaining key employees (70 per cent), increasing employee effectiveness (56 per cent), improving organisation reputation (48 per cent), improving business results (44 per cent), overcoming competitive pressure (38 per cent), other (3 per cent).

The refrain from the Work/Life professionals and their supporters is that everybody stands to benefit from policies to improve employees' work/life balance. Carol Muse Evans (2002), Associate Editor of the *Birmingham Family Times*, stakes the claim that: 'Businesses have found that family friendly policies lead to better balance, more creative and dedicated employees – workers who usually remain loyal to their employer, staying on the job year after year.' She states that companies are offering more-family-friendly programmes, policies, benefits and more – not only to help employees juggle work and family, but to lure good employees and keep them on the job year after year. A study presented at the British Psychological Society's 2001 annual conference reported that job sharing, and other flexible work arrangement such as flextime, reduced hours and working from home, could significantly improve performance. The report noted that managers of both job sharing and individual flexible workers rated these workers as providing a higher level of output than traditional full-time employees.

The availability of such practices is expected to expand. *Management Services* magazine (2000) published excerpts from a Hay Management Consultants survey of HR professionals in 123 UK organisations predicting that by the year 2005, 90 per cent of HR professionals expect that their organisations will be family friendly, with 53 per cent expecting that their organisations will allow flexible working hours (versus 23 per cent today) and 24 per cent predicting the provision of practical child-care support (for example crèches), versus only 10 per cent providing them today. Ten per cent expect their organisations to offer individually tailored solutions towards making employees' working lives easier (versus 1.7 per cent currently doing so). Further, 35 per cent of HR professionals expect that by 2005 their organisations will be offering employees a 'flexible benefit package' – a 'pick and mix' system whereby the employee chooses the appropriate benefits and doesn't receive others.

More than the provision of initiatives

Future-proofing the organisation requires more than just the provision of initiatives. In essence, future-proofing the organisation requires a shift in how employees (whether care-givers or not) are viewed.

> There is a huge amount of knowledge in any organisation. People at all levels have accumulated knowledge about what customers want, about how best to design products and processes, about what has worked in the past and what hasn't. A company that can collect that knowledge and share it between employees will have a huge advantage over an organisation that never discovers what its people know.
>
> (HRI, 2002)

Care-givers, with their irregular hours and focus on other commitments, are seen to be less relevant to the success of the organisation and are treated as such. But, they hold much valuable knowledge about the organisation that is easily lost and wasted. In order to prevent this they need to be seen as a capital asset and treated accordingly. As Drucker says:

> In no other area is the difference greater between manual-worker productivity and knowledge-worker productivity than in their respective economics. Economic theory and most business practice sees manual

workers as a cost. To be productive, knowledge-workers must be considered as a capital asset. Costs need to be controlled and reduced. Assets need to be made to grow.

(Drucker, 1999: 148)

Three main areas need to be addressed for this to happen:

1   care-giving and knowledge-management programmes need to be an intrinsic part of the organisational strategy;
2   human-resources and information-technology policies need to support the sharing of information;
3   the corporate culture needs to encourage a shift to share what is known and value individuals (whatever their care-giving status) as assets.

Incorporating policies into organisational strategy

For many organisations, the starting point for considering 'major innovations in work and employment' may well be found in the desire to acquire the 'best available talent'. Best available talent is likely to become the core of employer concern as national demographics point to a continual decline in the available talent pool.

Judging from interview responses from the executives detailed in Part II, some are approaching the work–life issues from the perspective 'anything that would allow us to have good people working on our books'. There seems to be recognition that it is in the organisation's best business interest to recruit and retain the best talent available. The catch is in defining the term 'available'. At present, as the empirical evidence shows, care-giving employees without the ability to regularly work extra hours and/or part-time employees are rarely included in the concept of 'best talent available'. In fact, survey evidence is that non-care-givers receive more management-development opportunities, full-time care-giver employees receive less and part-time employees receive little, if any. Granted, it has well justified employers' actions in limiting training investment to a selected few during periods of manpower surplus (most of recorded history). However, it is unlikely to continue to meet the needs of the organisation during the predicted prolonged periods of workforce shortage. In any event, the tension for organisations is in finding the balance between the cost of investment in developing the known talents of all employees, the cost of turnover and the cost of recruiting both new and replacement talent – of an unproven quality.

The cost of investment in developing the known talent of all employees may be offset against the longer-term benefits of retaining employees and retaining the good will of ex-employees. However, the desire to develop and support existing talent needs to be expressed at the level of organisational strategy. In other words, in order to maximise the unused potential of the talent represented by care-givers, organisations need to do more than just implement initiatives that are essentially offered (reactively) to ease the burden of support felt by care-givers.

By and large, the great majority of today's firms that have adopted family-friendly policies have reached that state through one of two routes: those firms focusing on the narrow child-care or women's issues have generally established a designated task force (or project champion) to guide the firm's child-care/women's-issues actions; and those firms focusing on the broader, more integrated, programmes such as flexible work arrangements have tended to put these into practice by employing a work–family administrator in the HR department. Critics charge that such well-intended (and even 'results-driven') efforts will miss the mark because they bypass the fundamental part played by corporate culture.

Voydanoff (1999) reports that both such organisational attempts ignore the fact that the organisational culture equates time and physical presence at work with productivity and commitment. The organisations view work–family problems as located in the family and of the employees', especially women's, own making. In this context, these programmes are associated with the separation of family from work, which undermines the efforts to achieve gender equity in the workplace, limits the use of the programmes by men, promotes a view that employee accommodations are a favour benefiting the employee rather than the organisation and places a stigma for participants in terms of their perceived commitment to the job. She advocates a search for a more holistic view of both the strategic interests of the organisation and the needs of employees.

We suggest that the organisation needs to proactively address and integrate its structures and policies in order to realise that strategy in full. Options include:

- reordering the work system so that employees can work longer hours at times not conflicting with care-giving responsibilities (flextime, compressed schedules – more hours, fewer days per week – work from home);
- reordering the care-provider system to augment the work-time resource of employees (improve availability, affordability and/or flexibility of care-provider arrangements);
- increasing employee earnings potential (resource gathering) from existing time availability (improve eligibility for promotion – obtain required talent at lower cost than promoting lesser talent or recruiting unproven talent).

The role of HR and IT

Each of the above options, and their integration into the organisational strategy, necessitates the key involvement of HR and IT. Both play an enabling role. As described in Chapter 10, the role of technology impacts in several ways. It enables workers to share knowledge and experience without limiting them to one location or time frame. It also enables the organisation to manage the financial and scheduling data associated with the employees' work lives in a way that would not have been feasible twenty years ago. The logistical and financial challenges of managing employees with unusual work patterns can be minimised by the use of appropriate systems. Such systems do, however, need to be integrated into the central core of management decision making if support for the irregular hours of care-givers (and others) is to become a central part of organisational strategy.

The role of HR as an enabler also needs to become a central part of organisational strategy. As a cautionary note, however, we are not suggesting that HR should necessarily be a centralised function. Indeed, the notion of future-proofing the organisation through adopting a flexible and knowledge-based approach would mitigate against such centralisation. Reich (2000) commented that the press of paid work tends to increase the regimentation of everything else and that the nature of work becomes less satisfying. Centralisation might well have a debilitating effect upon productivity. By suggesting that HR should become a central part of the organisation's strategy we mean that HR plays a crucial balancing role in meeting the needs of the organisation and the employees, and thus mediates and acts as a voice for all stakeholders.

The empirical evidence presented in Part II highlighted several areas in which HR mediation is vital. For example, as the nature of work changes and becomes more fluid, so job descriptions, which play an excellent part in a stable and more traditional organisational environment, become outdated. Some US respondents in particular talked of the job description as a job-limitation instrument. The role of HR in negotiating different forms of job description that allow flexibility in the timing, location and nature of the work that is undertaken, whilst also protecting the needs and rights of each of the stakeholders, will be vital and challenging.

Altering performance-assessment criteria

One aspect that impinges upon the HR role that came across particularly strongly in the empirical evidence was that of the way in which performance is assessed and rewarded. There is little need to belabour the point – long hours do not automatically equate to superior performance. Although we may not all like it, the tie between long hours and commitment is not quite so easy to dismiss. Long hours may not necessarily equate with commitment to the firm's success, but in the absence of some other standard, being 'Johnny/Janie-'on-the-spot', ready, willing and able to help' can be an easy surrogate for embattled supervisors trying their best to get the job done. Come performance-review time, most supervisors remember who was there when the going got tough. To many supervisors, performance-review time offers them an opportunity to show appreciation. That 'appreciation' turns into high marks and high marks frequently turn into promotion is more of a comment on the system than a criticism of the supervisor as a supervisor. In fact, when promotions are given, it signals more responsibility being given to the recipient and more investment about to be made in the recipient.

The organisation also wants that recipient to be committed to the organisation's success, and doesn't want to waste the upcoming investment on the promoted if that person is going to be short-termed or not sufficiently dedicated to getting the job done. Recall the Shakespearean edict: 'the fault lies not in our stars but in ourselves'. The tension for the organisation is in finding and implementing better approaches for determining true performance, better approaches for rewarding the faithful and better approaches for evaluating the commitment desired in those deemed to have promotion potential. None of the three will be easy, but separating the reward of the faithful from determining promotion-potential performance and promotion-required commitment to company success at least opens the door for those 'leave-on-time' care-givers, non-care-givers and part-timers to enhance their careers and for the organisation to realise additional gains from increasing utilisation of the best available talent pool.

Shifting the culture: flexible provision for all

Although HR and IT can play enabling roles, all the evidence points to the fact that without appropriate attitudes and values, commitment, motivation and involvement, the future-proofing of the organisation will be disjointed and inflexible. In other words, the organisation's culture, from the CEO to the lowest worker, needs to reflect and support the notion of flexible working.

The need for a supportive culture

Company policies designed to help employees integrate work and family roles do not, in and of themselves, reduce work/family conflict. Many studies have found that a supportive corporate culture is not only very important but a virtual key to the effort's success. Goff, Mount and Jamison (1990) concluded from their study of employer-supported child-care, work/family conflict and absenteeism that the more supportive the supervisor, the less work/family conflict experienced by the employee. In a telling article entitled 'Workplace culture fails to support work–life balance', Sally Dench, IES Senior Research fellow, makes the point that rights to time off and flexible working practices are not enough; that a change in culture and attitude within the organisation is necessary, and that both individuals and their managers need support to overcome real barriers. In noting that success in promoting work/life balance rarely occurs without positive leadership from above, the report highlights three keys for organisations seeking to achieve success in the work–life balance:

- the culture of the organisation must support, rather than deter, employees from achieving the work–life balance they need;
- managers must learn how to operate with teams that incorporate varied working patterns;
- employees must know what they can ask and how it can work.

Similarly, Linda Duxbury, a business professor at Carleton University, suggests that organisations need to alter their culture and the behaviour of their managers and supervisors to facilitate any form of permanent change. She insists that they have to measure progress and make managers accountable for progress in their areas. Organisations must remember that 'if it's not measured, it's not done'. She reports that supervisors act as gatekeepers to many of the benefits offered by the firm. Who you work for within an organisation has become more important than where you work. Employees who work for supportive supervisors who trust and respect them and who base their decisions on circumstances rather than 'the book' report less stress and greater productivity than employees who work for managers who deny them any sort of flexibility. Only one-third to one-half of the employees surveyed gave their managers high marks for their supportive behaviours.

The impact of the supervisor

Saltzstein, Ting and Saltzstein (2001) pinpoint a recurring theme from the literature: in many cases, workplace and societal cultures and expectations deter those most in need from even applying for such programmes and less than supportive supervisors undermine the benefits of specific programmes. This theme of a firm's culture being a barrier to implementing firm-approved work/life policies runs the gauntlet from employee reluctance to supervisors and managers being perceived as being less than supportive. Some typical observations were:

> Many people feel uncomfortable about asking for time off. They don't want to be seen as being needy. Employers may talk a lot about the need for work–life balance but some are workaholics – especially the senior management. In order to feel to be in the in-crowd, employees decide that that's what they have to do, too.
>
> (Lizotte, 2001)

Radcliff Public Policy Institute reports that too often, frontline managers convey the message, directly or indirectly, that flextime schedules create more work for them, or that they are uncomfortable with telecommuting because they prefer to have their staff members working where they can see them.

(Overman, 1999)

The Industrial Society's 2001 Worklife Report put it this way: 'The attitude and behaviour of managers is critical. A joke about 'part-timers' or a glance at a watch can undo a hundred HR policies on flexibility.' The IRS report also issued a most timely warning: 'not all workers want to work flexibly, some want to work nine to five. It is important to respect their choice, too'.

Director Richard Pearson, of the Institute for Employment Studies, sums up the challenge to the Human Resource professionals: 'Work life policies don't just kick in automatically. There are significant management, cultural and communications issues to resolve. A good employer will want the business benefits. Therefore they will want to know why take up is less than demand, and how they can provide the necessary leadership for change.'

The importance of the supervisors' attitude is supported by The Families and Work Institute's 1998 Business Work–Life Study. This reported on a survey of 1,057 companies – (84 per cent for-profit companies and 16 per cent non-profit companies) – with 100 or more employees and issued this 'Report Card' on the success of work/life implementation in the USA: Only 19 per cent felt that their supervisor made a 'real and ongoing effort to inform employees of available assistance for managing work and family responsibilities, and 56% felt that their supervisors did not successfully manage the work–family issues of employees in making job performance appraisals'. Finally, nearly 40 per cent of employees felt their careers would be negatively impacted if they took advantage of flexible schedules, or took time off for family reasons. It has already been noted that the major impediment to the uptake of existing initiatives designed to help care-givers is the attitude of the individual's line manager, and this was highlighted in the empirical evidence presented in Part II.

The negative effects of an unsympathetic supervisor can be balanced against the positive effects of a sympathetic one. Citing divergences between 'formal' and 'informal' organisational policies, Bourg and Segal (1999) point to these divergences as being an indicator of the importance of the individual supervisor's sensitivity and responsiveness. They cite research indicating that having a supportive supervisor is significantly related to increased schedule flexibility, higher job satisfaction, fewer serious problems with child-care, reduced work-to-home interface and reduced stress. Similarly, a Gallup (2000) study of 2 million employees at 700 companies found that most employees rate a caring boss higher than money and fringe benefits. Both tenure and productivity is determined by their relationship with their immediate supervisor. These findings confirm a 1999 Lou Harris Associates/Spherion poll that found that 40 per cent of those who rated their supervisor as 'poor' were likely to quit versus 11 per cent who rated their supervisor as 'excellent'. Littman (2002) summarised that employees stay because their managers create a place in which they want to be.

Such findings may give support to those who oppose legislated solutions to human problems (how do you 'legislate' good supervisors?) but they also bring a challenge to managers concerned with their 'bottom line'. Turnover is expensive and sensitive supervisors would appear to be a key. The focus by work/life advocates on the key role played by the immediate supervisor is not new to the companies. Their management-development and leadership-training activities have been focused on the immediate supervisor for years. Immediate supervisors are the key interface with employees in most operational activities of the organisation.

Summing up

In this chapter we have argued that in order to protect the organisation from the effects of the ageing population and technological change, both of which will lead to increased mobility and the need to retain staff, organisations need to adopt an integrated flexible approach to the work/life balance. Staff (whether care-givers or not) become a resource that can cost the organisation dearly if it is wasted; however, employees see the provision of a flexible system of programmes as a benefit, and such programmes enhance work/life and are believed to be economically effective.

Although firms increasing the availability of work–family benefits to their employees may be anticipating an increase in productivity, little more than anecdotal evidence supports this expectation. For most employers, creditable financial analysis will be required for winning the support of line management for those work–life initiatives that appear to meet the firm's self-interest.

Work–life balance programmes, however, need to be fully incorporated into the organisations' strategic plans, and integrated (particularly) with the HR and IT functions. The main future-proofing, though, is one of attitudes and behaviours, such that line managers are fully supportive of those seeking ways around the work/life balance.

Attending to the needs of care-givers now can help insure the future of the organisation – however, both individuals and organisations are located within the State, and their futures are entwined. The organisation is affected not just by the legislation aimed at it but also by the way in which the State legislates for the individual employee. These threads will be addressed in the next chapter.

13 Tensions for the state

This chapter follows on from the previous three in this part by looking at the role the State plays (or might play) in the support of care-giving, and the implications of this. Chapter 10 outlined two different care-giving-related responses to the challenge of the ageing population. These two approaches are characterised by the USA and the UK, who, though very similar in many things, present subtle differences in policy and practice that impact upon where the responsibility for supporting care-givers is assumed to be located. The chapter then moves on to explore the long-term strategy in relation to changing demographics and the need to foster developments in the labour force and support national wealth.

National significance of changing demographics

Chapter 10 argued that across the world there are few nations who are retaining their birth-rate at replacement level, and that in the vast majority the population level is falling dramatically. It has been projected that for every hundred working-age persons in 1988 there were nineteen retired persons. The prediction is that by 2010 this will rise to twenty-two retired per hundred working, and by 2050 to thirty-eight retired persons per hundred working-age persons. Overhanging the debate on child-care-giving are the predictions of dramatic change in population demographics signalling that the demands for elder-care will continue to rise steadily in the twenty-first century (Marchese, Bassham and Ryan, 2002). Decisions that are made now about how best to support care-givers might have a profound effect upon the rate of drop in the birth-rate, as well as set the economic, social and political parameters of the nation for the future.

This dual effect harks back to Pearce's (2002) argument, which suggests a strong link between a reduction or cessation of the rate of decline in birth-rate and sufficient support for care-givers such that they are able to hold down a successful career whilst also raising a family and/or providing care for the elderly. Pearce based his argument on State support systems. Drucker (1999), working from a similar data base, suggested that organisations in association with a mobile and immigrant workforce would be able to provide the necessary flexibility to maintain the US birth rate. In either case, the State needs to ensure that there are systems in place to secure a sufficient and active workforce in future generations.

The balance that is obtained between the role of the State and that of the organisation in the support of care-givers will also affect (and be affected by) the nature of work and the extent to which organisations have been future-proofed against the demands of a reduced working population that is supporting an elderly general population. The State's quandary is: 'How do we maintain our standard of living if we have too few human resources to maintain our national productivity and our global competitive position?' (Little and Triest, 2002).

Over the course of the coming years, much debate is likely to take place over the 'how'. Some things will have to be done differently if the multiple effects of the projected collapsing birth-rate are to be modified or eliminated. Not all of the potential effects of a declining birth-rate can be calculated in advance. For those effects that can be estimated, there is unlikely to be universal agreement on either the estimate itself or the appropriate response to the estimated effect. However, one response to the question of resource utilisation – especially human resources utilisation – is appropriate for almost any projected birth-rate situation, whether collapsing or bulging. Both individual and society are best served when resources are not wasted. Care-givers who are passed over for promotion and who receive less training and do not achieve their career potential are a wasted resource. We will briefly examine existing State provision for the support of care-giving, before looking at some wider policy-related issues.

Overview of US/UK legislation with reference to care-giving

The UK government's adoption of the EU social charter and other EU directives has led to significant legislation. This includes the working-time directive, which limits working hours and lays down minimum annual leave, the part-time workers directive, which gives equal rights to part-timers, and the parental leave legislation, which gives both parents rights to time off to spend at home with their children (McCurry, 2000).

Following the EU's example, the UK passed the Employment Act of 2002, which contains a number of provisions designed to enhance the rights of working parents. The Act includes provisions for:

- 6 months' paid and a further 6 months' unpaid maternity leave for working mothers;
- 2 weeks' paid paternity leave for working fathers;
- 6 months' paid and a further 6 months' unpaid leave for a working

adoptive parent, providing the employee has 26 weeks' continuous service into the week in which they are notified by an approved adoption agency of being matched with a child for adoption;

- an increase in the rate of statutory maternity pay from £75 per week to £100 per week from April 2003 or to 90 per cent of average weekly earnings if this is less than £100;

- reimbursement of 92 per cent of the costs of maternity, paternity and adoptive payments under the Statutory Maternity Pay (Compensation of Employers) Amendment Regulations 2002 (SI 2002/225), which came into effect on April 6, 2002. Small employers (defined as those whose annual National Insurance payments are £40,000 or under) are now able to recover 104.5 per cent of these costs;

- employees with children under the age of 6, or under 18 if the child is disabled, having the right to request flexible working arrangements providing they have 26 weeks' continuous service at the date of application. Flexible working arrangements cover a range of options, including a change in hours of work, the times of work or the place of work (request to work from home). The purpose of the request must be to enable the employee to care for a child under the age of 6 years, or under 18 years if the child is disabled.

From April 2003, nearly 6 million families will be eligible to claim the new Child Tax Credit, which replaces the current Children's Tax Credit and Working Families' Tax Credit. Lower-income families will receive an enhanced benefit, and elements of needs-based philosophy reduce the benefits to higher income families (Homedad.org. May 21, 2002).

In the USA the situation has a different slant. With the passage of the Family Leave Act (FMLA) in 1992, workers who have worked at least 1,250 hours over the preceding year with firms having fifty employees or more within a 75 mile radius of one of their worksites were granted rights to 12 weeks of unpaid, job-protected leave each year for childbirth, adoption, foster-care placement, a serious medical condition or care of a child or spouse with a serious medical condition. (Some families receive varying periods of paid leave through employer-based disability benefits. The 1998 Business Work–Life Study by Families and Work Institute reports that 53 per cent of companies provided some replacement pay for maternity leave, 13 per cent for paternity leave and 12.5 per cent for adoption/ foster-care leave.) Several federal programmes support child-care or related services, primarily for low-income working families. In addition the tax code includes provisions specifically targeted to assist families with child-care expenses. Examples of major programme highlights of US federal government assistance in the child-care area are provided in the Congressional Research Service: *Child Care in the 107th Congress* (updated May 21, 2002):

- Child Care and Development Block Grant (CCDBG), which was created in 1990 and expanded in 1996. The CCDBG provides block grants to states, according to a formula, that are used to subsidise the child-care expenses of families with children under the age of 13, if the parents are working or in school and family income is less than 85 per cent of the state median. Child-care services are provided on a sliding fee-scale basis, and parents may choose to receive assistance through vouchers or certificates, which can be used with a provider of the parent's choice, including sectarian providers and relatives.
- Temporary Assistance for Needy Families (TANF). This act provides fixed block grants for state-designed programmes of time-limited and work-conditioned aid to families with children. Child-care is one of the services for which states may use TANF funding.
- Child and Adult Care Food Program provides federal funds for meals and snacks served in licensed child-care centres, family and group care homes, and Head Start centres. Eligible providers are usually public and non-profit organisations.
- Head Start provides comprehensive early-childhood education and development services to low-income preschool children, typically (but not always) on a part-time basis.
- Individuals with Disabilities Education Act programmes authorise an early intervention programme for infants and toddlers with disabilities and their families and preschool grants for children with disabilities.
- Loan forgiveness for child-care providers, contained in amendments to the 1998 Higher Education Act, provides that borrowers who have earned a degree in early-childhood education and work for 2 years as a child provider in a low-income community may have a portion of their loan obligation forgiven.
- Child Care Access Means Parents in School, under the Higher Education Act of 1998 amendments, supports the participation of low-income parents in post-secondary education through campus-based child-care services.
- Dependent Care Tax Credit is a non-refundable tax credit for employment-related expenses incurred for the care of a dependant child under the age of 13 or a disabled dependant spouse. The tax credit rate is gradually reduced from 30 per cent to 20 per cent as incomes go up for taxpayers with income above US$10,000. The 2003 Economic Growth and Economic and Tax Reconciliation Act similarly reduces the tax credit allowed for children's expenses from 35 per cent for taxpayers with adjusted gross income of less than US$15,000 to 20 per cent for taxpayers with income above US$43,000.
- Dependent Care Assistance Program. Under the tax code, payments made by a taxpayer's employer for dependant-care assistance may be excluded from the employee's income and therefore not be subject to federal income tax or employment taxes.

Five states provide Public Disability Insurance programmes. Because the Pregnancy Discrimination Act applies to these programmes, new mothers have the right to short periods of paid leave if they have either private or public disability benefits. The 1998 Business Work–Life Study reported that 23 per cent of companies employing 100 or more workers provided elder-care resource and referral services. Only 9 per cent offered long-term care insurance for family members, with another 12 per cent actively considering the insurance.

Forty-two states currently have some form of pre-kindergarten services. In June 2000, the US Department of Labor issued regulations that allow states to extend unemployment insurance to mothers out of work by virtue of childbirth.

As has been previously noted, the UK adopts a more communitarian approach to child-care and currently has more generous child-care support for parents than does the USA. However, it does not presently approach the higher level of benefits offered by its European neighbours. As a member of the European Union and having recently signed on to the EU's Social Charter, it is arguable whether the question of 'who pays whom' in the work/life debate will receive similar answers in the halls of UK and US governments.

Core of dilemma: 'who pays for whom?'

Chapter 11 focused on care-givers who are trying to weave their way between the growing expectation of society that all adults should be working and the historical expectation for women to shoulder the primary responsibility for caring in the home. The increasing participation of males in the care-giving process was also noted, as were the existence of high 'outside' priorities of many non-care-giver employees. Chapter 12 focused on organisations. Organisations need to make a profit to survive, yet need to balance this against future-proofing – expending money on support for care-givers (and others) now in order to continue to survive. Both look to the State, as the third main stakeholder in this conundrum, for support, though, at present, they seek different forms of support.

Gornick and Meyers (2001) point out that in the USA, parents are struggling to find private solutions to this 'who will care for the children' problem but some feel that private solutions only exacerbate gender equality, overburden the parents and, ultimately, lead to poor-quality child-care. Gornick and Meyers list and comment upon several of the private solutions being used by many US parents:

1   combining parental care-giving with part-time employment. Noting that only 42 per cent of American women work full time, it is con-cluded that this part-time solution falls overwhelmingly on women and thus exacerbates gender inequality in both the workplace and the

caring spheres and the after effects contribute to wage penalties that persist long after the children are grown;

2   combining substitute care for children with full-time parental employment. Noting that 44 per cent of children below 1 year old are now in some form of non-parental child-care, it is concluded that this solution places a heavy financial burden on parents and raises concern about the quality of care in the children's youngest and most developmentally sensitive years;

3   impoverishing a large, low-wage child-care workforce dominated by women. They note that child-care workers in the USA are among the poorest paid, usually without benefits or opportunities of career advancement, and poorly educated.

This view urges US policy makers to take a cue from the European welfare states, which finance extensive parental leave during the earliest years of children's lives and provide high-quality early-childhood education and care services for older children. They view the role model as two Scandinavian countries that have consolidated maternity, paternity and other parental-leave schemes. Norwegian parents are entitled to share 52 weeks of leave with an 80 per cent wage replacement (or 42 week at full wage replacement) following the birth of a child, while Swedish parents can share a full year of leave with nearly full wage replacement, followed by an additional 3 months at a lower rate. Gornick and Meyers (2001) admit, however, that US resistance to lessons that could be learned from overseas have been fuelled by vivid press reports of the collapse of the European welfare states.

Opposition to this view of state child-care facilities and generous payments that benefit working parents is encouraged by the political arithmetic encompassed in the US statistic that the majority of workers do not have children under the age of 18 (Young, 1999). Further, Voydanoff (1999) reminds that the USA tends toward individualism, family self-determination and a residual role for the State regarding work and family issues. She holds that these ideologies have important implications for public policy and corporate policies and programmes. US opponents of European-style parental leave point out that parental leave is actually taken by less than 10 per cent of the eligible fathers across the European welfare states but is overwhelmingly taken by mothers. This has led to the observation that despite the greater state support for care-givers in the UK, many women continue to pay a price for their long absences from the workplace in the form of lost human capital and career advancement. Conversely, literature review and survey/interview comments reveal that many proclaim that not all mothers, or even the majority of mothers, wish to pursue a career and many prefer their primary role to be that of homemaker.

The Institute of Management Services (Anonymous 2002c) comments that public policy (UK) encourages women to be involved in the labour market whether or not they have children. Commenting that almost half of the UK's lone mothers are now in some sort of paid work, the Institute noted that paid work is increasingly seen as the salvation of all, with governments switching from paying benefits to people not working towards a 'workfare' type system that emphasises that people have responsibilities as well as rights.

This view is supported by Helen Wilkinson (2001), who suggests that reinventing child-care as a business opportunity might be a good strategy both for parents and the economy. She points out that demand for qualified child-care workers was expected by the government's Childcare Commission in 2001 to exceed 300,000 over the next 4 years. She maintains that the cost of child-care is prohibitive for many working parents (who typically bear 93 per cent of the cost burden), that employers have been absent from the child-care debate because government policy has not encouraged and rewarded family-friendly employers and that both large and small child-care entrepreneurs have not received the support needed to grow their businesses. Wilkinson advocates that child-care be thought of as a public good – like an effective transportation system – rather than as a burden that the taxpayers bear. She proposes that the national child-care strategy be recognised as a business opportunity for growing a new industry both meeting the needs of working parents and providing employment for care providers.

Both the US and the UK governments have focused upon the waste of talent within the workforce associated with the need for child-care. The USA has looked more to the individuals and the organisations to meet the needs of the workforce, whilst the UK has sought to support these needs through greater legislation. Neither has yet fully come to terms with the increasing need for elder-care, nor the need to support the future-proofing of organisations, as discussed in the previous chapter.

Having said that, it should be remembered that calls for the State to lead are not necessarily calls for the State to legislate. In fact, it could be argued that the role of government is to create the environment for change rather than to dictate the change itself. Governments have the ability via creating incentives and disincentives to cause both individuals and corporations to alter their behaviour in the direction desired by national policy. Leadership includes establishing, facilitating and assisting the dialogue for determining national consensus as well as legislating when required. The empirical evidence and discussion of the literature presented earlier in this book indicate several areas in which such state leadership might be beneficial.

Need to support national wealth

Both the UK and US governments (along with most governments across the world) have the improvement of the standard of living of their inhabitants as their continuing goal. That they may approach the same problems (opportunities) from different directions or seek similar or dissimilar solutions should come as no surprise. Leaving aside the individualism/communitarianism biases in the underlying philosophy of the two countries, the tensions emanating from the population demographic projections being experienced by the two States are similar in several areas pertinent to this study, although the degree of each tension being experienced by the State may and does vary.

Regardless of whether it is achieved by supporting individuals directly or by encouraging organisations to help carry the burden of such support, it is the responsibility of government to ensure that sufficient national policy, supported by legislation and incentives where appropriate, are in place to encourage all who wish to further their career to do so to the maximum of their potential, regardless of their circumstances. As the empirical evidence presented in Part 2 indicates, whilst much of the literature focuses upon the gender-discriminatory problems associated with child-care, the problems of male care-givers and of those who provide elder-care have not received the same attention. The State, therefore, needs to ensure that these less-recognised groups are also included and supported in the national dialogue.

Organisations play a key role in securing national wealth, and the relationship between organisations and the State is full of challenges – not least in terms of balancing state support for growth against the policing of malpractice. Whilst the wastage of human talent could be seen as ethically circumspect it could rarely be classed as malpractice and so it might seem appropriate to denote pressure from individual care-givers as the driver for organisational change. Indeed, as argued in the previous chapter, there is every indication that it is in the organisation's best long-term interest to train and retain all its employees, to seek integrated flexible systems of working and to foster change in attitudes and behaviour such that the organisation is better able to meet the challenges associated with demographic and technological changes in the future. In those organisations that are far-seeing and alert, pressure for change might well come as they scan the environment. However, the urgency of demographic change and the speed of technological change mean that organisations need to be changing now, and it falls to the State to help them recognise that need and to provide structures and incentives in support of such change. The argument for state support in this area is simple – it is the best way to ensure the long-term economic and social health of the State. This can be seen in several key areas, outlined below.

Education

Leadership from the State is needed to ensure that the talents of its population are developed to their full potential. The more limited the supply of human resources, the greater the need (and effort required) to bring available resources to full potential. Improving education availability and content has long been a priority for both governments. The empirical evidence in Part II would seem to indicate that care-giving affects educational attainment as well as career progression. The two are, of course, entwined: whilst the organisations can be encouraged to provide more work-related training and development, the State must take some responsibility for ensuring that the basic educational needs of its populace are met. More needs to be done to make education accessible to the disadvantaged care-giver and to make it manageable when balanced against the demands of work and care-giving.

Employment

Leadership is needed to ensure that the talents of the population are utilised to a degree that satisfies both society's needs and society's desires and/or tolerance. The evidence supplied by the literature generally and by this empirical study specifically would indicate that additional talented yet untapped human resources currently exist for filling some of the expected void. Specific issues arising from this research into care-giving/career progression for which the State's intervention may be invited are working opportunities for care-givers who seek greater flexibility in working hours, training, promotion opportunities, and greater recognition of the emotional and financial burdens of parents (female and male) and counter-demands from those whose choice was not to assume the burdens.

Mobility

Mobility of the population is a factor deserving to be kept under close watch – particularly in the UK, where family care-providers are still in the majority and turnover has yet to reach US rates. If population trends continue as currently projected, an increase in mobility of the population may accompany a general population decrease as talent shortages in specific regions drive up the commercial value of employee talent. If the population in general or the knowledge worker in particular becomes more mobile – moving to areas offering the most opportunity – the need for care-provider facilities will increase as the availability of extended-family care-providers will have been left behind in the old neighbourhoods. Recall that 61 per cent of UK respondent care-giver employees used unpaid care-providers. The need for non-family care-providers is likely to rise and demands for more state involvement may become more insistent.

Benchmarking

As the workforce becomes more mobile and the nature of work more flexible, there will be an increasing need for benchmarking or comparability of qualifications, attainment and provision. For example, the UK has national systems of vocational and non-vocational qualifications, and systems of rating higher and further educational provision, and in this way qualifications become portable benefits – the individual is not tied to company-specific training and the organisation knows the exact standards the individual has achieved. Such national systems do have their problems, and it is beyond the scope of this book to address the debate directly. This example is used, however, to illustrate that as flexibility and mobility become more central to the nature of work, so does the ability to make sound judgements about the comparability of different elements. Another example, mentioned in the previous chapters, is that of evaluating or rating care facilities for those care-givers who wish to subcontract but who do not have the knowledge or facilities to undertake such assessment themselves.

Professionalisation

As geographical and organisational boundaries lose their rigidity, people are increasingly turning to their professional bodies to enhance their sense of identity at work and provide a sense of permanence. After all, an individual is likely to be a member of one or more professional bodies all their working life but may only be with a single organisation for a few years. Professional bodies, therefore, are likely to become more vocal champions of their members' needs and rights. They are also in a position to collaborate with, or act as mediator between, the organisation, the individual and the State. Professional bodies are in a position to support the State in developing leadership on many of the issues associated with care-giving and can, for example, be encouraged to take the lead in such things as benchmarking. There is some tension here, as some professional bodies have a tendency towards empire building and demarcation. It therefore behoves the State and the professional bodies to seek to collaborate in co-creating the future.

Migration, immigration and 'virtual' migration/immigration

The shifting demographics and erosion of geographical and organisational boundaries means that when an organisation seeks to use the best talent available it can access such talent across the world in a piecemeal way. Similarly, individuals from one location can be working in many others at the same time. We are moving into an era of physical migration and immigration (as people move to chase jobs and organisations attract employees from other countries) and also *virtual* migration and immigration. The social and political consequences of this have only just started to impact upon nations and have yet to be fully faced. There are also economic challenges. The State needs to find ways to tax and manage a highly mobile workforce that works, as needed, in other countries and that includes work from non-nationals on a piecemeal and irregular basis. Parts of such work, especially the technology-related parts, might also be hard to trace. Work-based contributions to the national wealth such as employment tax might well be hard to administer.

Summing up

In this chapter we have explored the role that the State can play in supporting care-givers, and we have argued that such support is essential to the national wealth. We have outlined the global challenge of the ageing population and have presented two possible ways forward that are, in essence, being adopted by the USA and the UK. They are not directly comparable and are moulded by differing concepts of agency. It is likely that they will produce different outcomes. Governments have a large incentive for encouraging those things which better develop and utilise the talents of their populations (both present and future) – that of supporting national wealth whilst enhancing social health. Included in providing the atmosphere for continuing productivity improvement would be updating skills for national competitiveness and providing incentives and disincentives to industry to steer their activities in those directions that minimise waste of resources, particularly human resources.

14 Conclusions

In this chapter we conclude our task. Care-giving and its effect upon careers has been shown to be both more complex than is often acknowledged – in that the impact of care-giving on career is situation specific and has far-reaching consequences – and also more simple – in that these issues are not gender specific. To our knowledge, no empirical study designed to attempt to verify the underlying causes, if any, of the effects of care-giving on career development and progression is known to have been published. Specifically, none is known to exist within the banking industry. The pinpointing of the essential role played by the freedom to pursue career (home-base coverage) has also not previously been exposed in the literature.

The root causes of the wastage of human resource must be made known – one by one – if the developed world is to marshal its resources to counteract the effects of the declining birth-rate. This book presents empirical evidence to demonstrate care-giving's debilitating effect upon the best use of available talent in the organisation. No country, however developed or rich, can afford to under-utilise its assets. There is growing recognition that a country's human resources are at least as important to its development as its natural resources. Not all – or even the majority – of the employed in the UK and the USA are care-givers. The interests of non-care-givers must also be given weight in the search for achieving a better balance within our lives. And the *sine qua non*, the enablers – the companies and the State – must also benefit from any re-engineering of the structure and nature of work if there is to be lasting progress for the human aspect of production. One thing is certain: this care-giver talent pool has much to offer and is being under-utilised. In the light of projected future talent shortage, will care-giving be the 'glass ceiling' that retards human progress in the new millennium?

Overview of the argument

This book provides empirical evidence of the effect of one priority (care-giving) upon another (work). Society has placed a high priority on the care of its children and elders. Society has also placed a high priority on that activity which supports self, family, organisation and nation – work. The pressures and structures of modern living have increased the need for more of the able-bodied to perform remunerative work (usually outside of the home) but have not relieved the need of children and elders to rely on others for their care.

Females as well as males have career aspirations and males as well as females have care-giving responsibilities. However, not all (or even the majority of) employees have care-giving responsibilities. The issue of fairness to all employees becomes entangled. Further, for the majority of organisations, an employer's first duty to both employees and community is to be a profitable concern, capable of providing, at minimum, sustained employment for existing employees. States seek an ever-increasing standard of living for their inhabitants. Democratic governments must not only seek and lead consensus among the governed but they must do so within the framework of the demographic and technological challenges being presented at the dawn of the twenty-first century.

Having set the stage, Chapter 2 opened the analysis by providing the background for the emergence of care-giving as a career constraint. Historically viewed as 'women's work', care-giving was briefly reviewed by the chapter in the context of the feminist movement's progress as it sought recognition of women's home responsibilities (and contributions) via the domestic labour debate, the patriarchy debate and the discrimination and 'glass ceiling' debates. Chapter 3 moved forward to concentrate the debate on care-giving, chronicling the evolution of the division of labour, reviewing UK and US workforce demographics, the growing male role with care-giving, the roles played by 'choice' (agency), and the differing views between the UK and the USA about the role adopted by the State in support for care-giving. Chapter 4 took this further, presenting empirical data gathered during a small (135 UK and US respondents) survey of lone parents, which showed that the impact of care-giving upon job careers was gender free in both the UK and the USA.

The second part presented the main empirical research upon which the views expressed in this book are founded. Chapter 5 briefly detailed the research population and the methodology adopted. Chapter 6 explored the interrelationship between care-giving and the perceptions of commitment required for receiving promotions and/or the development opportunities leading to promotion. Demonstrating the required commitment is perceived as being synonymous with the ability to work 'long hours'. Evidence was presented that employees unencumbered by care-giving responsibilities work more hours per week and can positively respond more frequently to requests to work extra hours. Chapter 7 reviewed the evidence comparing care-giver employees with non-care-giver employees in development-opportunity areas such as participation in formal development programmes, management training, mentors and performance appraisal. Chapter 8 reviewed the evidence surrounding job-level attainment of care-givers and non-care-givers. Chapter 9 concluded that those employees that have others providing adequate and prompt support for their dependants have 'time freedom' to pursue their careers and are better able to progress in their careers – whether male or female.

The third part built upon the first two and examined the findings in relation to the debates outlined earlier. Chapter 10 set the stage by examining projections for the collapsing birth-rate and the demographic changes taking place in the UK and US workforces. It then introduced and discussed some of the initiatives collectively known as 'work/life' balance issues. Chapter 11 examined some of the tensions that the present structure of work and living are creating for the individual – both care-giver and non-care-giver – employees. Chapter 12 explored some of the tensions to be experienced by the companies as they examine work/life issues and projected talent shortage. Chapter 13 looked at potential tensions for the State arising from recent demographic changes that have taken place in the national workforce and projections of shortage in the future national workforce.

The qualitative data showed conclusively that an employee needs to put in long hours and be available at short notice in order to appear committed to his or her job, and that this is a prerequisite for full-time status, career development and promotion. Both females and males expressed these views, and there was a complete absence of any dissenting voice in this. Keeping in mind the adopted definition of 'glass ceiling' (as an upper limit to professional advancement that – though openly perceived – is not openly acknowledged), the equating of career progression to long hours that care-givers by nature of their responsibility are unable to supply becomes an aspect of the glass ceiling. As the lack of acknowledgement of care-giving's effect pertains to male as well as female limitation on professional advancement, care-giving does indeed present a gender neutral glass ceiling.

Are the questions answered?

At the outset some basic questions were posed about care-giving and its effects that have been left unanswered in the literature. Based on this research, we feel that some insights have been obtained. We certainly do not claim to have all the answers, but do propose some tentative conclusions.

Does care-giving affect career?

Based on the evidence from the empirical research presented in Part II, we conclude that the time spent in care-giving is such that the time available for pursuing career ambitions is more limited for the care-giver than for the person unencumbered by care-giving responsibilities. Our evidence confirms the perception of employees that long hours are required in order to be considered sufficiently committed to merit promotion. It's a matter of 'is home-base covered?' – is someone else providing the required care and leaving the employee with the 'time freedom' to pursue a career. The evidence shows that those who do have home-base covered generally achieve higher levels within the organisation than those who do not.

Who is being adversely affected?

Chapter 4, all of Part II and Chapter 11 show that those employees with primary care-giver responsibilities – generally, those employees with children living in the same household under the age of 18, or those with elderly dependants needing daily care – are adversely affected as the time required to fulfil these obligations reduces the time available to pursue career objectives. Both males and females are impacted. The research shows that care-giving responsibilities are gender neutral. The cultures of both the UK and the USA assign the primary care responsibility much more frequently to women than to men and so a greater number of females are impacted than men. However, in the case of married or partnered households it is a family decision that assigns primary care responsibility, which can go to either partner, be shared or be subcontracted, either to paid employees or external providers, or family and friends. In the single-parent household there is no family decision to make – the lone parent has no one with whom to share the responsibility. Lone parents, of course, can be either female or male, and their only option is to devote their time to their care-giving responsibilities or seek outside support. In each case, the empirical data showed that care-giving responsibilities take precedence over work and career opportunities.

What effects does care-giving have on the organisation?

Chapters 10 and 12 addressed this issue. The full effects of time-limitations/stress being experienced by employees with care-giving responsibilities upon the organisations that employ them are not fully known to date. It is only within more recent times, with the demise of the traditional 'breadwinner' family model and the re-emergence of the feminist movement, that the spotlight of public awareness has been cast upon the role played by care-giving in the modern work environment. There is much anecdotal evidence and some emerging case studies that raise the spectre of adverse effects being experienced by employing organisations: increased absenteeism, higher turnover, reduced productivity, increased health risk, and more being attributed to the care-giving responsibilities of employees. More recently, the positive effects of initiatives designed to counter the advertised adverse effects of care-giving (for example, family-friendly/work–life policies) have been receiving some attention in the literature, such as increased productivity, greater recruitment potential and so on. To date, most of the positive claims have been supported primarily by anecdotal evidence and frequently comes from sources that could be considered as having a favourable bias.

It may be logical to expect that there will be adverse cost effects for the employer from the stresses being experienced by the care-giver and that these adverse effects might manifest themselves in higher absenteeism, turnover, and other voluntary and involuntary reactions to the care-giver's 'time bind'. More recently, there seems to be recognition that there might also be some adverse effects from the non-care-giver on the employers who administer the well-intended care-giver medicine of family-friendly policies. The postulations of positive effects for the employer from heralded work–life fatigue counter-measures must be considered as remaining in the realm of speculation as the needed cost studies have rarely been attempted to verify the anecdotal evidence offered by the initiatives' supporters.

To date, there seems to be a decided dearth of 'hard facts' to support either the 'logical' expectations of adverse cost effects or the potential for the positive effect of counter-measures. The answer to the key question of what effects care-giving have on the organisation must remain in the 'don't know' category. However, unless and until creditable answers are found, especially to those questions addressing the positive effects, it is not hard to predict that the enthusiastic embracing of work–life balance measures by employers will be equivocal.

If we look to the future, and the impact that the ageing population and technological changes might have upon organisations and the nature of work, then the evidence, as it stands, suggests that the nature and location of work will change, and that issues associated with care-giving will increasingly impact upon an organisation's sustainability. We speculate that organisations need to be putting into place integrated and flexible policies and practices now in order to create a future-proof profile.

Are there primary causes for adverse effects of care-giving on career?

The evidence seems clear though the remedies seem daunting. 'Long hours' are almost universally perceived as being required of those serious about career advancement. The empirical evidence produced from the surveys and executive interviews undertaken for this research confirms both the perception and the reality. 'Long hours' seem deeply imbedded in business culture as being a key affirmation of a promotion-candidate's 'commitment' to the success of the company, and a person's commitment to company success is usually a fundamental requirement for promotion. Flowing from the 'long hour' syndrome is the evidence of employer reluctance to invest in developmental activities for those not meeting the minimum requirements to be deemed committed – part-time employees and full-time employees with care-giving responsibilities who either have no partner or whose partner works full time. For a discussion of the need to reform performance-assessment criteria, please see Chapter 12. We suggest that the need to address this bias in evaluating an individual's contribution to the organisation is central in addressing the situation, but that it is so deeply rooted in many organisations that a culture change is vital. Such a change would, in particular, need to address the often 'unconvinced' attitudes of the line managers and encourage care-givers to seek more flexible working patterns.

Are there options available?

There are, and these are mainly discussed in Chapters 3, 12 and 13. As with any attempts to meet newly recognised challenges, many alternatives have been proposed, some have been adopted for trial, few have been in practice long enough to be fully evaluated. Initial proposals quite naturally come from those being adversely affected by the perceived injustice, but counter-proposals, or a backlash, have come from those being adversely affected by the remedies proposed by the initial group. Initially, the concerns of the care-giver group were responded to by employers beginning to implement 'family friendly' policies, especially where the employer evaluated a 'win/win' situation as presenting itself. More recently, a group of initiatives collectively known as work/life balance has gained centre stage in line with the views of the majority of employees – those unencumbered by care-giving concerns. A plethora of options is presently available, the more successful of which will be those that show promise of meeting the challenge and delivering improvements for all parties with a stake in the outcome.

Whose responsibility is it to support care-giving?

We have reviewed the differing approaches for evaluating 'family concerns' in terms generally attributable to the more communitarian predisposition of the UK and the more individualist predisposition of the USA in Chapters 3 and 13. It is not our task to 'take sides' in this debate. What is appropriate, however, is to point out that although the debate may have started with family concerns, it has now broadened to recognise that work and life are inseparable from each other and that all employees – care-givers and non-care-givers alike – must grapple with the priorities to be accorded to the many time-demanding activities required and/or desired in life.

Earlier chapters in this part look at the three main stakeholders in the care-giving conundrum – the individual, the organisation and the State (and introduce a fourth in Chapter 13, the professional bodies). Each has much to gain from supporting the role of the care-giver, and each bears some costs. We suggest that none has sole responsibility, but that it is in the best interests of each to work together to provide the legislation, leadership, policies, practices and changes in attitudes and behaviour necessary to make full use of what is, at present, wasted human talent.

The resolution of this conundrum, the way in which the stakeholders' costs and benefits are balanced, will be different for different national cultures, and will depend, in part, upon where agency is seen to be located. We are moving into an era of human resource shortage and it is undeniable that some resolution needs to be reached, and that the way in which it is reached, the form of balance that is achieved, will have a profound effect upon the future of the nation, the nature of the organisation and the reality of the work/life balance for the individual.

What is fair – and fair to whom?

To determine 'fair to whom' would require that we possess unusual insight into the eyes of the many beholders. We have no such ability. However, there are some broad requirements of fairness that might be stated for the employee/employer relationship. It would seem that an appropriate test of fairness must meet the needs of three constituents:

- *individual employee* – in her or his own self-interest, each individual wants to feel valued as a person and that her or his own needs/wants/desires are taken into consideration by the employer;
- *workforce* – in their self-interest, employees want to feel that no one of them receives special (favourable) treatment that is not available to the others of like talent or work location/group;
- *company* – in its self-interest, the company prefers employees to feel that they are being treated fairly because there is evidence to show that such employees generate greater productive effort than comes from employees who feel they are being treated unfairly. The self-interest of the company is grounded in the knowledge that productive effort from employees is required for the company to reach its goal of survival/prosperity.

What is 'fair' is, of course, very subjective. While not pretty, such a three-party basic test of fairness might be helpful in crafting and implementing initiatives that seek to improve the structure of work as it is practised today.

Challenges for human resource professionals

As discussed in Chapter 12, it is to the human resource professional that we must look in balancing the tensions around what is fair and to whom, the information necessary for strategic planning on behalf of the organisation and the State, and thus for leadership in the continuing quest for advancing the total contribution of the human element of production. The HR professional sits at the interface between the individuals and the organisation, and has (or can acquire) the knowledge and resources to gather data and influence organisational strategy. The HR profession, as a body, is in a similar position to work with, and influence the relationship between, organisations and the State. HR is the mediator that can help all parties work together to meet the challenges of the twenty-first century. Based on the research and findings of this study, which complements much of the existing literature yet brings some new perspectives, some of the highlighted issues challenging the human resource professionals are outlined below.

Performance-assessment criteria/loyalty/commitment

From the literature comes this advice: 'Performance Appraisals should reflect results achieved, not hours spent.' While not disagreeing with this common-sense advice for redirecting the basis of employee performance evaluation, we feel it oversimplifies the problem as it does not adequately address the root causes of the present situation. Please see Chapter 12 for background. The 'results-not-hours' approach to the long-hour syndrome (perhaps the major contributor in current evaluation schemes) appears to us to neglect the perplexity of the supervising evaluator's situation, namely:

- the difficulty of determining individual responsibility for results achieved;
- the ease of determining who is around to help when I need it;
- the desire to reward (and encourage to continue) persons whom I can rely on; and
- the need for a benchmark in order to determine the commitment needed for promotion.

The challenge to HR is far more than just devising better tools to determine the results achieved. It is to find, convince and implement new and appropriate ways of helping the supervisor reward reliability/loyalty (to himself or herself and to the company) and to define and implement a system for better identifying the attributes of commitment necessary for promotion. As these fall into place, it will be easier to get the supervising evaluator's attention to the vital task of appropriately evaluating results.

Culture change required

We add our small voice to the chorus that challenges HR to lead the cultural change that is required to foster the 'results not hours' approach. However, we advise caution in over-reliance on the mantra that 'change must be visible at the top'. As was evident in Part II, the problems associated with the need to care for dependants impact and are resolved differently at different organisational levels. What must be visible is the positive concern of top management for the priorities of the individual and the positive evidence that results are what get recognition. Top management sets the tone of the organisation. Over-reliance on creating time-based behaviour change in highly motivated and driven top management both denies those individuals the activities they may actually prefer and is setting up a time frame for cultural change success that might be unnecessarily long – if not actually setting up top management for the 'fall guy' role. What is needed is an integrated and flexible response that meets the aims of the culture change whilst recognising and supporting the various needs and ways of working adopted by different individuals.

Work/life

By whatever name, this book confirms that employees with primary care-giving responsibilities are under time-compression constraints as they seek to do the work of the employer yet must accord pride of place to the needs of their families. In recognising their first priority to be family caring and given the 'traditional' time-structure approach to work utilised by most employers, the time available for achieving both their employer's desires and their own career aspirations is necessarily more limited than for the employee who is unencumbered by care-giving responsibilities. The result of this has led to the talents of care-giver employees being under-utilised and thus the acceptance of a lower level of overall productivity than could be accomplished in a less stressful environment.

Initially, HR rose to meet this challenge by fostering the installation of 'family-friendly' policies. However, these policies show evidence of failing to meet the test of fairness for the majority of employees, the non-care-givers. Responding to this newer challenge, HR has spearheaded the broader, more inclusive, 'work/life' set of initiatives that feature flexibility focused on both the needs of the individual and the needs of the work group of like talent/group/location. Primary candidates for flexibility encompass both the issues of available-time allocation between company and non-company priorities (flexible schedules, flexible location, flexible job-content initiatives and so on) and the issue of tailoring benefits to individual employees' needs within a framework of equity for all employees in the distribution of available company benefit funding (cafeteria benefit plans, for example).

Despite these, the empirical evidence shows that the majority of employees with care-giving responsibilities continue to fail to make full use of the opportunities available to them, many of which remain as peripheral additions to the functioning of the organisation. HR's challenge is to mediate between the stakeholders such that the flexible working associated with care-giving becomes an integral part of the working of the organisation, and to lead the search for proving (or disproving) fairness of the various proposed initiatives for the companies.

Costing – and leadership for consensus

For work/life initiatives to reach their potential, they must both pass the three-party test of fairness and be proven to help the organisation's sustainability. Much of the cost/benefit analysis that has been presented to date can be viewed as coming from sources that either display the potential for a 'conflict of interest' (for example work/life advocates, affected-worker surveys) or have relied upon anecdotal evidence from those untrained in the rigour of cost/benefit analysis. Granted, cost/benefit analysis is difficult in areas with so much subjective data, but CFOs understand the costs of turnover and absenteeism, and CEOs understand that greater productivity means more output for less input. Such 'hard proof' will be hard to achieve, but this is the challenge – especially for HR. These new and/or yet-to-be-discovered work/life techniques will not produce the same results for all companies. They may not produce the same results even within the same company – some operations or departments may benefit strongly whilst in others the same initiative may even be a drag on the operation. The real challenge, however, will be in driving the consensus on what constitutes creditable cost data. The range of data points is large. Much may not 'fit' within conventional cost-data collection systems. As HR carries the responsibility for advancing the contribution of the human element of production, the 'driver for cost/benefit consensus' must be the HR professional.

A call for further research

As the future unfolds, additional research will need to urgently establish those areas for 'major innovations in work and employment' called for by Drucker (1999), and associated with predictions of an ageing population and technological change.

The research in this book focused on the service sector of the economy, specifically the research was limited to the UK/US banking sector. This sector employs a higher female-to-total employment ratio than does the manufacturing sector. Replication of the study in the manufacturing sector would confirm/reject the applicability of the findings to that sector.

Quantitative data in Part II shows the USA to be more reliant on paid care (contract care) and the UK on unpaid care (presumably family care). The US tendency to rely more on paid than unpaid care-providers may have more to do with less availability of extended family than it has with the more ready availability of paid resources. The lack of care-giving facilities was a frequent complaint from the UK lone parent survey (Chapter 4) that was echoed by some of the primary survey respondents. There is some evidence that the US care-giver prefers family care-providers. Further research into the making available of care-provider facilities is needed in both countries in order to provide a better informa-tion base for those seeking solutions for the improved utilisation of care-giver talents.

There is a pervasive perception that 'long hours' equates to evidence of commitment, which is required to gain career development and promo-tion opportunities, and HR specialists confirm that the tendency exists. Further research is needed to verify the contention and to explore avenues for improving performance-evaluation assessment approaches.

The potential for a 'backlash' to family-friendly policies from non-care-givers was noted in the literature and several of the comments presented here. If this is a real phenomenon, then it indicates that policies that are essentially well intentioned might be counter-productive. Further research is needed to establish the extent to which the backlash exists.

Care-giver tenure generally exceeds non-care-giver tenure in length of company service. Why? Do the reasons have relevance for improving the use of available talent? Are there unrecognised cost benefits accruing to this longer tenure? This is another area into which further research is needed.

Much anecdotal evidence is filling the media – both pro and con – on family-friendly policies and work–life balance. There is a need for more research to confirm or refute the tie between these policies and turnover/absenteeism reduction/productivity. For lasting change in the approach to 'work within the realities of life', creditable cost-analysis tech-niques for investigating the complex effects of this tie need to be researched and implemented.

Final comment

Overhanging the debate on child care-giving are the predictions of dra-matic change in population demographics that signal that the demands for elder-care will continue to rise steadily in the twenty-first century. *The England Economic Review* (2002, first quarter) comments that to many observers one particularly challenging issue is how a relatively small work-force will supply the consumption needs of a growing number of depen-dants without a decline in UK living standards. Increased productivity provides one obvious answer. New approaches to work are required to keep governments on the path of providing continuing improvement in their citizens' standard of living. The required new approaches to work must be placed on the table, debated, prototyped, refined and adopted sooner rather than later. It's time we take that first giant step for mankind *now*.

In a strange twist of fate, the core arguments of the domestic labour debate of the 1960s may belatedly find a berth at the national level of debate on the plummeting birth-rates and its potential effects on the standard of living as its core agenda of advocating pay for the domestic tasks performed by women (including the caring tasks) becomes pertinent again. Antonell Picchio (2000) decried the lack of a clearer and more direct focus on the process of social reproduction of labour and the conflict between profits and the standard of living of the labouring population. She concluded: 'What is treated as a women's issue is in fact a fundamental problem in the system.'

As the keeper of the collective will of its citizens, a major goal of democratic governments is to nurture national economic productivity whilst satisfying the national conscience. Nowhere does this challenge become more manifest than in the employment arena. It is in the employment arena that the national need for its businesses to be competitive meets the businesses' need for productive employees and both business and nation meet the employees' need for acceptable lifestyles. A nation aspires to retain and enhance the standard of living for its people, yet to produce a national economic output requires resources inputs – land, labour and capital (in constantly varying proportions). In view of the population demographic projections for the nations of the developed world, there will be insufficient labour within most, and possibly all, of these individual nations both to produce the desired standard of living and to do so within the present structure and practices of society within these individual nations.

The almost uniform projections for the individual developed nations is for birth-rates below replacement rate, leading to an ageing population, and thus to a lesser number of workers (lesser input implied) supporting an increasing number of elderly retirees (greater output consumed). To maintain (let alone increase) the standard of living of a nation under these circumstances requires a substantial adjustment to the present labour productivity (input/hour) currently being experienced in these countries. Input can be increased either by increasing the number of future workers or by increasing future worker productivity, or by some combination of the two. In the absence of increased input, output must decrease – and so too the standard of living of the nation.

Increasing the number of workers can take several directions: more of the nation's future population can come into the workforce, more hours per working person can be committed, or more immigration from other nations can be allowed (or, to same effect, more goods can be imported from other nations). Increasing future worker productivity can be accomplished either by increasing capital spending to 'automate' more output from each worker or by introducing new non-capital approaches for encouraging more output from existing available resource input. In actuality, the dramatic changes projected in population demographics will be likely to require the fullest exploration of all available avenues for increasing input to match the required increase in output. No nation will willingly accept the alternative – the lowering of output – the lowering of its citizens standard of living.

To date, the major, high-profiled (and increasingly contentious) approach of developed countries for increasing population (and securing greater amounts of productive resources) has been to encourage increases in immigration. The US Immigration and Naturalization Service (INS) estimates suggest that roughly 35 per cent of the growth in the US population in the 1990s was due to immigration – a contribution not seen in the USA since the early 1900s (Little and Triest, 2002). Immigration is a time tested and proven technique for increasing national population, creativity, productivity. In spite of its drawbacks and at times ill-concealed lack of political popularity, it has a place in each developed nation's strategy for maintaining/increasing national productivity.

Each nation of the developed world utilises the market economy as its engine for producing the national output (gross domestic product – GDP). The for-profit sector of the economy is the mainstay of the market economy. Self-interest drives the competitive spirit that has produced the business environment needed for each nation to attain the status of a developed country. It is primarily in the house of the private sector that the parameters of the employment arena for tomorrow's workers will be designed, prototyped and perfected. It is here that the future input/output ratios will be birthed. To effect those 'major innovations in work and employment' called for by Drucker (1999) will require 'buy in' by the private sector and its employees – present and potential. Along with other creative innovations for improving the input side of the productivity equation that may still be on the drawing boards of the future, a number of emerging techniques are already being attempted for increasing both the size and the productivity of the existing workforce.

Technological changes are already leading to virtual immigration, in which parcels of work are outsourced across the world. Whilst this avoids some of the nationalistic issues associated with immigration, it will present governments and organisations with serious challenges. There will be an increasing mismatch between their workforce and their citizenry, with the resulting need for increased information gathering and what might be seen as intrusion into the individual's privacy in order to tax and manage a highly mobile workforce.

Side by side with immigration (real and virtual), major innovations in work and employment, in both the UK and the USA, have been taking place in the 'work/life' area. The need is to find 'win/win/win' – new arrangements that bring greater satisfaction to both employees and potential employees whilst strengthening the competitive position of the companies and the nations. Some of the newer techniques show great promise of delivering this ideal – the anecdotal evidence is mounting. Whilst 'hard-numbers' evidence is difficult to produce and is therefore scarce, the soft evidence supporting the bottom-line results of some of the newer techniques is consistent and uniformly favourable, sometimes in spite of the operational difficulties inherent in implementing some of the techniques. On the other hand, some other techniques appear to support the greater-satisfaction side of the equation whilst neglecting the financially competitive side.

Having attractive work/life policies is one thing. Having employees feel comfortable in utilising them is another. The key seems to be in the organisation's culture, especially where the culture is perceived as sending the signal that making use of work/life opportunities is a request for 'career death'. Yet pressure is continuing to mount for a better work/life balance. The growing number of employers adopting some form of work/life programmes is indicative that employers as well as employees recognise that those caught up in the conflict between parenting and being good employees may be less productive than they otherwise could be.

We believe that the empirical evidence set forth in this book has made the case that care-giving to date has been shown to be a detriment to the career progression of employees. We believe that the non-work-connected restraints placed on the time-freedom of care-givers to pursue their careers is wasting a national resource that could help mitigate the effects of a diminishing worker population. We believe that the interests of all workers must be given full consideration in the design and implementation of any new initiatives for increasing the availability and the productivity of all employees – including the majority of employees without care-giving responsibilities. The reality of fairness includes the perception of fairness for all. There is no 'silver bullet' to cure all conflicts between work and life, work/life programmes notwithstanding. But there are major gains that can – and must – be made if we are to continue to enjoy the national standard of living to which the developed world has become accustomed.

This book ends on the note that it began: 'the most important new certainty is the collapsing birth rate of the developed world' (Drucker, 1999). The developed world cannot afford to waste its dwindling human resources. The old saying 'waste not, want not' is familiar to most. The projected birth-rates give added incentive to eliminate any wastage presently being experienced by the non-utilisation of willing care-giver talent. Each nation has a vital stake in improving its own standard of living.

Our progress as nations and as individuals requires continual improvement in the process of completing the daily task of living.

(Drucker, 1999)

This book provides empirical evidence of human resource wastage – a need has been identified and should be met. Meeting it requires the co-operation of individuals, companies and the State. The global decline in birth-rate challenges us to get on with the job of eliminating this wastage of our most precious resource – the human being.

References

Ackroyd, S. and Fleetwood, S. (2000). *Realist Perspectives on Management and Organisations*, London: Routledge.

Alliance of Work/Life Professionals (2002). 'Use of work/life benefits on the rise', *Human Resources and Compensation e-Library*, (accessed 1 August 2002). Available at: http://www.ioma/managementlibrary.com

Anonymous (1994). 'Statistical feature', *Employment Gazette*, (UK) Government Statistical Service, April: 111.

Anonymous (2000). 'Labour market and family status of women, not seasonally adjusted, November 2000', *Labour Market Trends*, 108, 11: 6.

Anonymous (2002a). 'Appeals court rejects custody for house-husbands', Home Dad.org.uk, Tuesday, 21 May.

Anonymous (2002b). 'Better deal for British workers by 2005, says new survey', *Management Services Magazine*, 44, 19: 4.

Anonymous (2002c). 'Workplace culture fails to support work life balance', *Management Services*, Staffordshire: Institute of Management Services, 46, 6, June: 6.

Armstrong, M. (1995). 'Diversity with a difference', *Credit World*, 85, 5: 32–5.

Baizer, C. (2001). *Business and HR: The link at the bottom line*, Westport, CT: Quorum Books.

Barnes, B. (2001). 'The macro-micro problem, and structure and agency', in Ritze, G. and Smart, B. (eds) *Handbook of Social Theory*, London: Sage, pp. 345–50.

Barnett, R. (1999). 'A new work-life model for the twenty-first century', *Annals of the American Academy of Political and Social Science*, 562: 143–59.

Barrett, M. (1995). 'Dual-earner dads may be the latest victims of salary discrimination', *Academy of Management*, 9, 32: 71–2.

Becker, P. and Moen, P. (1999). 'Scaling back: Dual-earner couples' work-family strategies', *Journal of Marriage and the Family*, 61, 4: 995.

Bertrand, M. and Hallock, K. (2002). 'The gender trap in top corporate jobs', *The Wilson Quarterly Review*, 16, 1: 89.

Billings, Y. and Alvesson, M. (1992). 'Gender and organisation: Towards a differentiated understanding', *Organization Studies*, 13, 1: 73–103.

Blau, F. and Beller, A. (1998). 'Trends in earnings differential by gender, 1971–1981', *Industrial and Labor Relations Review*, 41: 513–29.

Bourg, C. and Segal, M. (1999). 'The impact of family supportive policies and practices on organizational commitment to the Army', *Armed Forces and Society*, 25, 4: 633–52.

Boyacigiller, N. and Adler, N. (1991). 'The parochial dinosaur: Organisational science in a global context', *Academy of Management Review*, 16, 2: 262–90.

Boyd, R. (2003). 'Study: Grandmothers crucial in evolution', *The Birmingham (Alabama) News*, 2 February: 9A.

Brannen, J. (1999). 'Caring for children', in Walby, S. (ed.) *New Agendas for Women*, Basingstoke: Macmillan Press Ltd, p. 51.

Brannen, J. and Moss, P. (1993). *Managing Mothers: Dual earner households after maternity leave*, London: Unwin Hyman, p. 34.

British Bankers' Association. (2001). http://www.bba.org.uk (accessed 2001).

Brown, D.B. (2002). *Evaluating Human Capital*, London: Chartered Institute of Personnel and Development.

Browne, A. (1998). 'A bonnet for baby. Why new mothers are hurrying back to the labour force', *Observer*, 19 July: Business, p. 1.

Bruegel, I. (2000). 'The restructuring of the family wage system, wage relations and gender', in Clarke, L., de Gijsel, P. and Janssen, J. (eds), *The Dynamics of Wage Relations in the New Europe*, Boston, MA: Kluwer Academic Publishers, pp. 9–29.

Bubeck, D. (1995). *Care, Gender, and Justice*, Oxford: Clarendon Press, p. 215.

Burkett, E. (2000). *The Baby Boom: How family-friendly America cheats the childless*, New York, NY: The Free Press.

Burton, C. (1985). *Subordination. Feminism and social theory*, Sydney: George Allen & Unwin.

Chandler, T., Kamo, Y. and Werbel, J. (1994). 'Do delays in marriage and child birth affect earnings?', *Social Science Quarterly*, 75, December: 838–53.

CIPD (1999). *Knowledge Management: A literature review*, London: Chartered Institute of Personnel and Development.

Clarksberg, M. and Moen, P. (2000). 'The Time Squeeze: The mismatch between work-hour patterns and preferences'. Unpublished manuscript.

Cohn, S. (1996). 'Human capital theory', in Dubeck, P. and Borman, K. (eds) *Women and Work: A handbook*, New York: Garland Publishing, Inc., p. 107.

Congressional Research Service (US): RL30944: Child care issues in the 107th Congress (updated 21 May, 2002).

Coyle, D. (1996). 'The wage gap leaves women in part-time ghettos', *Independent*, 21 March: 24.

Coyne, B. (2001). Care-giving: a gender neutral 'glass ceiling'? Ph.D. Thesis. Lancaster: Department of Behaviour in Organisations, Lancaster University, October.

Davidson, M. and Cooper, C. (1993). *European Women in Business and Management*, London: Paul Chapman Publishing Ltd, p. 16.

Dench, S. (2002). 'Workplace culture fails to support work–life balance', *Management Services*, 46, 6: 6.

Dillner, L. (2000). 'Women: Battle of the bulge', *Manchester Guardian*, 19 July: 2.

Dolliver, M. (2000). 'Marching into battle: Parent vs. non-parents', *Adweek – Eastern Division*, 41, 11: 32.

Doughty, S. (1996). 'Divorce's dismal record as four in ten marriages fail', *Daily Mail*, 20 March: 2.

Doyle, J. (2001). 'Time out – the case for time sovereignty', *Worklife Report 2001*, 13, 3: 11.

Drucker, P. (1999). *Management challenges for the 21st Century*. New York: Harper-Collins Publishers, Inc., p. 44.

Dunkel, T. (1996). 'The front runners', *Working Women*, April: 30–6.

The Economist (1996). *A wealth of working women*, 8 June: 27–8.

The Economist (1998a). *For better, for worse*, 18 July: 3–14.

The Economist (1998b). *A gentle invasion*, 18–24 July: 6–9.

The Economist (2002). *Half a billion Americans?* 24 August: 22.

The Economist (2003). *Pocket World in Figures, 2003 Edition*, London: Profile Books Ltd.

Estrich, S. (1996). 'Women drop out, why can't men, too?', *USA Today*, 14 March: 12A.

Evans, C. (2002). 'Family friendly companies have loyal employees', *Best Companies for Working Families*, Seventh Annual Edition, Birmingham Family Times, Birmingham, AL: United Parenting Publications.

Fandray, D. (2000). 'What is work/life worth?', *Workforce*, 79, 5: 64.

Felmlee, D.H. 1984. 'The dynamics of women's job mobility' *Work and Occupations*, 11: 259–81.

Fields, M. (2001). *Indispensable employees, How to hire them and how to keep them*, Franklin Lakes, NJ: Career Press.

Fitzgerald, S. (2001). *The Birmingham (Alabama) News*, April 19: 8A.

Flynn, G. (1996). 'Deloitte & Touche change women's minds', *Personnel Journal*, 75, 4: 56–68.

French, M. (1993). *The War Against Women*, New York: Ballantine Books, p. 14.

Frey, Jennifer (2000). 'Steinem's "I do" at 66 surprises, elates pals', *The Washington Post* in *The Birmingham News*, September 12: E5.

Friedman, D. (1998). 'Help Wanted', *The McKinsey Quarterly*, 1: 41.

Fuchs, V. (1989). 'Women's quest for economic equality', *Journal of Economic Perspectives*: 25–41.

Galinsky E., Bond, J. and Friedman, D. (1993). *The Changing Work Force: Highlights of the National Study*, New York: Families and Work Institute.

Galloway, B. (2001). Family Assistance Administrator, Public Assistance Office, Department of Human Resources, State of Alabama, Jefferson County, Alabama. Personal interview by B.S. Coyne on 14 June.

Gardiner, J. (1997). *Gender, Care, and Economics*, Basingstoke: Macmillan Press, pp. 82–125.

Gerbman, R. (2000). 'Elder carer takes America by storm', *HR Magazine*, 45, 5: 50–8.

Giddens, A. (1997). *Sociology*, 3rd edn, Cambridge, UK: Polity Press.

Giddens, A. (1993). *New Rules of Sociological Method*, Cambridge: Polity Press.

Glickman, L. (1997). *A Living Wage: American workers and the making of consumer society*, Ithaca, NY: Cornell University Press.

Goff, S., Mount, K. and Jamison, R. (1990). 'Employer supported child care, work/family conflict, and absenteeism: A field study', *Personnel Journal*, 43: 793–809.

Golden, L. (1997). 'Working time and the impact of policy initiatives. Reforming the overtime hours law and regulations', *Review of Social Economy*, 61: 522–41.

Gornick, C. and Meyers, M. (2001). 'Support for working families', *The American Prospect*, 1 January, 12, 1: S3.

Gray, J. (1997). 'The fall in men's return to marriage: Declining productivity effects or changing selection?', *Journal of Human Resources*, 32: 481–504.

Grover, M. (1999). 'Daddy stress', *Forbes*, 164, 5: 202.

Gutek, A. and Larwood, L. (1987). 'Introduction: Women careers are important and different.' in Gutek, B.A. and Larwood, L. (eds), *Women's Career Development* Newbury Park, CA: Sage.

Hakim, C. (1996). *Key Issues in Women's Work. Female heterogeneity and the polarisation of women's employment,* London: The Athlone Press Ltd.

Hale, E. (2000). 'The greying of Europe: Economies in jeopardy', *USA Today,* 22 December: 14A.

Hampton-Turner, C. and Trompenaars, F. (1993). *The Seven Cultures of Capitalism,* London: Judy Piakus Ltd, p. 14.

Han, S. and Moen, P. (1999). 'Work and family over time: A life course approach', *Annals of the American Academy of Political and Social Science,* 562: 98–111.

Hasslette, B., Geis, F. and Carter, M. (1992). *Organisational Women: Power and paradox,* New Jersey: Ablex Publishing Corporation, p. 35.

Hewitt Associates (1999). *1999 survey of US employers,* Lincolnshire, IL: Hewitt Associates.

Hill, R. (1993). 'Women and work – is the glass ceiling coming down?', *Risk Management,* 40, 7: 26–34.

Hirsh, W. and Jackson, C. (1993). *Women into Management,* Institute of Manpower Studies, Report P158, 9: 55.

Hobson, C., Delunas, L. and Kesic, D. (2001). 'Compelling evidence of the need for corporate work/life balance initiatives: results from a national survey of stressful life-events', *Journal of Employment Counseling,* 38, 1.

Hochchild, A. (1997). *The Second Shift,* New York: Avon Books.

Hofstede, G. (1980). *Culture's Consequences,* London: Sage.

Hofstede, G. (1983). 'National cultures in four dimensions', *International Studies of Management and Organization,* 13, 2: 52.

Hordern, B. (1996). 'Women in the middle – menopause and the sandwich generation', *Seasons,* 6, 2: 8.

Houston Chronicle (2000). 'Workplace changes/mothers with small children pioneering flexibility for all', 25 September: 18.

Howe, E. and McRea, S. (1992). 'Women on the board', *Policy Institute Studies,* London: Policy Institute Studies: 4.

Human Resources Institute (2000). 'Measuring the impact of caregiving responsibilities in the labor force: Employer Perspective', St Petersburg, FL: University of Tampa Press (http://www.hrinstitute.info).

Humm, M. (ed.) (1992). *Modern Feminists – Political, Literary, Cultural,* New York: Columbia University Press, p. 406.

Jackson, B. (2000). 'Gender-wage gap decided by more than discrimination', *CNN* (http://www.cnn.com/2000/US/05/10/gender/bender), 10 May.

Jackson, M. (1996). 'Women still hit barriers in boardroom, survey says', *The Sun Sentinel,* Ft. Lauderdale, FL: The Sun Sentinel Company, p. 1D.

Jamrog, J. (2001). 'The changing nature of work, people and HR', Human Resources Institute, St Petersburg, FL: University of Tampa Press.

Jones, C. and Causer, G. (1995). 'Men don't have families: Equality and motherhood in technical employment', *Gender, Work and Organisation,* 2, 2: 51–62.

Kane, M. (2002). 'Dads piece together sick days, vacation for undercover leave', *The Birmingham (Alabama) News,* 16 June, Sec E: 1.

Kelly, R. (1991). *The Gendered Economy.* London: Sage Publications, p. 32.

Kleiman, C. (1996). 'Glass ceiling panel should be resurrected', *The Sun-Sentinel – Weekly Business*. Ft. Lauderdale, Florida: Sun-Sentinel Publishing Co., January 15, p.19.

Korenman, S. and Neumark, D. (1991). 'Does marriage really make men more productive?', *Journal of Human Resources*, 26: 282–307.

Kossek, E., Colquitt, J. and Noe, R. (2001). 'Caregiving decisions, wellbeing, and performance: The effects of place and provider as a function of dependant type and work-family climates', *Academy of Management Journal*, February: 39.

Large, M. and Saunders, M. (1995). 'A decision making model for analysing how the glass ceiling is maintained: unblocking equal promotion opportunities', *International Journal of Career Management*, 7, 2: 21–8.

Lee, K. (2000). 'Eldercare benefits are gaining more attention', *Employee Benefits News*, 1 May.

Leonard, B. (1996). 'Long hours, hard work can break the glass ceiling', *HR Magazine*, 41, 4: 4.

Lewis, S. (2001). 'Restructuring workplace cultures: The ultimate work–family challenge', *Women in Management Review*, 16, 1: 21–9.

Little, J. and Triest, R. (2002). 'The impact of demographic change on U.S. labor markets', *New England Economic Review*, 1st Quarter: 47–69.

Littman, M. (2002). 'Best bosses tell all', *Working Women*, October: 48.

Lizotte, K. (2001). 'Are balance benefits for real?', *Journal of Business Strategy*, 22, 2: 32.

Loh, E. (1996). 'Productivity differences and the marriage wage premium for white males', *Journal of Human Resources*, 31, 566–89.

Long, J. (1990). 'The origins of sex differences in science', *Social Forces*, 68: 1297–315.

McClelland, D.C. (1988). *Human Motivation*, Cambridge, UK: Cambridge University Press.

McCurry, P. (2002). 'Getting the balance right', *Employee Benefits*, Centaur Publishing, October: S6.

Mack, T. (2000). 'In Britain, who'll mind the kids?', *USA Today*, 12 July: 12A.

McKenna, E. (1997). *When Work Doesn't Work Anymore*, New York, NY: Delecorte Press.

McQuarrie, F. (1994). 'Are women set up for failure on the road to the executive suite?', *The Academy of Management Executive Magazine*, 8, 4: 84.

Marchese, M., Bassham, G. and Ryan, J. (2002). 'Work-family conflict: A virtue ethics analysis', *Journal of Business Ethics*, 40, 2: 145–54.

Meyer, C., Mukerjee, S. and Sestero, A. (2001). 'Work-family benefits: Which ones maximize profits', *Journal of Managerial Issues*, 13, 1: 28–44.

Mies, M. (1986). *Patriarchy and Accumulation on a World Scale*, London: Zed Books.

Moen, P. and Yu, Y. (2000). 'Effective work–life strategies: Working couples, work conditions, gender, and life quality', *Social Problems*, 47, 3: 291.

Moore, T. (1996). 'Home is the housewife's choice', *Daily Telegraph*, London, 22 April: 7.

Morgan, P. (1996). 'Who needs parents? The effects of childcare and early education on children in Britain and the USA', *Choice in Welfare Series*, No. 31, Institute of Economic Affairs.

Noe, R., Hollenbeck, J., Gerhart, B. and Wright, P. (1997). *Human Resources Management: Gaining a competitive advantage*, Homewood, IL: Irwin, p. 408.

Overman, S. (1999). 'Make family-friendly initiatives fly', *HR Focus*, 76, 7: 1.

Pearce, F. (2002). 'Mamma Mia', *New Scientist*, 20 July: 38–41.

Picchio, A. (2000). 'Wages as a reflection of socially embedded production and reproduction processes', in Clark, L., de Gijsel, P. and Janssen, J. (eds) *The Dynamics of Wage Relations in the New Europe*, The Netherlands: Kluwer Academic Publishers, p. 196

Poe, A. (2000). 'The baby blues', *HR Magazine*, 45, 7: 78–84.

Popenoe, D. (1996). *Life Without Father*. New York: The Free Press, pp. 2–6.

Powell, G. and Butterfield, A. (1994). 'Investigating the "glass ceiling" phenomenon: An empirical study of actual promotions to top management', *Academy of Management Journal*, 37, 1: 68–86.

Ragins, B. and Sundstrom, E. (1989). 'Gender and power in organisations.' *Psychological Bulletin*, 105: 51–88.

Rasberry, W. (2000). 'Mothers hating necessary compromises of child care', *The Birmingham News*, 28 August: 7A.

Reich, R.B. (2000). *The Future of Success*, New York: Random House, p. 171.

Reingold, J. (1999). 'Why your workers might jump ship', *Business Week*, 1 March: 0.8.

Robinson, J. and Godbey, G. (1997). *Time for Life: The surprising ways Americans use their lives*, University Park, PA: Penn State Press.

Rodgers, F. and Rodgers, C. (1989). 'The business and the fact of family life', *Harvard Business Review*, November–December: 121–9.

Rosin, H. and Korabik, K. (1990). 'Marital and family correlates of women manager's attrition from organisations' *Journal of Vocational Behavior*, 37: 104–20.

Rubin, B. (2003). 'Many hop off the "Mommy Track"', *The Birmingham (Alabama) News*, 1 January: 2E.

Saltzstein, A., Ting, Y. and Saltzstein, G. (2001). 'Work–life balance and job satisfaction: The impact of family friendly policies on attitudes of federal government employees', *Public Administration Review*, 61, 4: 452–67.

Scarritt, T. (2002). 'More women needed in leadership positions', Commentary, *The Birmingham (Alabama) News*, 17 March: Sec C: 1.

Schadovitz, D. (1996). 'A glass half empty', *Human Resources Executive Magazine*, 10, 5: 7.

Schwartz, F. (1989). 'Management women and the new facts of life', *Harvard Business Review*, 71: 65–76.

Schwartz, F. (1992). 'Women as a business imperative', *Harvard Business Review*, March–April: 106–13.

Schwartz, F. (1996). 'The competitive advantage', *Journal of Accountancy*, 181, 2: 39.

Scott, C. (1997). 'Yes Mrs. Horlick, we can have it all ... but we don't want it', *Sunday Times*: 'Focus', 21 September: 18.

Sherman, A., Bohlander, G. and Snell, S. (1998). *Managing Human Resources*, Cincinatti: South-Western.

Shore, R. (1998). *Ahead of the curve: Why America's leading employers are addressing the needs of new and expectant parents*, New York: Families and Work Institute.

Skapinker, M. (2002). *Knowledge Management: The change agenda*, London: Chartered Institute of Personnel and Development.

Taylor, N. (2002). *Getting a Kick Out of Work: Survey report*, London: Chartered Institute of Personnel and Development.

Taylor, T. (1997). 'Class matters, "race" matters, gender matters', in Mahony, P. and Zmroczek, C. (eds) *Working-class Women's Perspectives on Social Class*, London: Taylor & Francis.

Taylor Nelson Sofres, http:www.tns-global.com.

Thomas Jr, R. (1990). 'From affirmative action to affirming diversity', *Harvard Business Review*, March–April: 107–17.

Treanor, J. (2001). 'Boost for women in fight for equal pay', Careers, Society-Guardian.co.uk@Guardian newspapers limited, 6 December, 2001.

Tsui, A. and Gutek, B. (1984). 'A role set analysis of gender differences in performance, affective relationships, and gender success of middle managers', *Academy of Management*, 23, 3: 619–35.

US Budget For Fiscal Year 2003, Department of Health and Human Resources: 156–64.

US Census Bureau (1996). 'Projected number of families with children under 18', Series #1 estimates, May.

US Census Bureau (1997a). *Current Population Reports*, September.

US Census Bureau (1997b). 'My daddy takes care of me! Fathers as care providers', *Current Population Reports, Home Economics Studies*, September: 70–59.

US Census Bureau (2000). *Child Support for Custodial Mothers and Fathers*, October.

US Department of Commerce, Economics and Statistics Administration, Bureau of the Census (1994). 'Who's minding the kids?', Statistical Brief, April.

US Department of Labor, Bureau of Labor Statistics (2003). 'Civilian labor force by sex, age, race, and Hispanic origin, 1990, 2000, and projected 2010. Table 5.

US Equal Employment Opportunity Commission (1999). *Aggregate Report for Depository Institutions*, (http:www.eeoc.gov/ststs/jobpat/1999/sic60.html).

Voydanoff, P. (1999). *National Council on Family Relations*, Minneapolis, MN: April.

Waldfogel, J. (1997). 'The effect of children on women's wages', *American Sociological Review*, 62: 209–17

Ward, L., (2001). 'New law "to give 400,000 more parents flexible hours"', Society-Guardian.co.uk@Guardian Newspapers Limited, Careers, 20 November.

Warren, T., Rowlingson, K. and Whyley, C. (2001). 'Female finances: Gender wage gaps and gender asset gaps', *Work, Employment and Society*, 15, 3: 465.

Webster's College Dictionary (1991). New York: Random House.

Weiers, Ronald M. (2002). *Business Statistics*, 4th Edn. London: Thompson Learning, p. 123.

Wilkinson, H. (2001). *Crèche Barriers: How Britain can grow its child care industry*, London: Genderquake and Demos.

Wilson, R. (1996). 'A defense of working mothers', *The Chronicle of Higher Education*, 16 May: A-5.

Woodall, J. and Winstanley, D. (1998). *Management Development – Strategy and Practice*, Oxford: Blackwell Publishers, p. 223.

Worrell, L. and Cooper, G. (1999). *Quality of Life: 1999 survey of managers' changing experience*, London: Institute of Management.

Wright Investor's Services (2001). http.//www.wisi.com (accessed 2001).

Young, M. (1999). 'Work–family backlash: Begging the question, what's fair?', *The Annals of American Academy of Political Science*, March: 32, 1.

Young, Mary (1997). *What's Behind Work/Family Backlash? 1997 Research report with recommendations for practice*, New York: Center for Workforce Strategies, p. 1.

Index

eBooks – at www.eBookstore.tandf.co.uk

A library at your fingertips!

eBooks are electronic versions of printed books. You can store them on your PC/laptop or browse them online.

They have advantages for anyone needing rapid access to a wide variety of published, copyright information.

eBooks can help your research by enabling you to bookmark chapters, annotate text and use instant searches to find specific words or phrases. Several eBook files would fit on even a small laptop or PDA.

NEW: Save money by eSubscribing: cheap, online access to any eBook for as long as you need it.

Annual subscription packages

We now offer special low-cost bulk subscriptions to packages of eBooks in certain subject areas. These are available to libraries or to individuals.

For more information please contact webmaster.ebooks@tandf.co.uk

We're continually developing the eBook concept, so keep up to date by visiting the website.

www.eBookstore.tandf.co.uk